STUDIES ON THE SONG CELESTIAL

REVIEW OF THE TRANSLATION OF THE BHAGAVADGITA (THE SONG OF CELESTIAL) BY SIR EDWIN ARNOLD

SWAMI SOUMYANANDA

Made with ♥ on the Notion Press Platform
www.notionpress.com

This study is dedicated to fellow aspirants having willingness to study Indian Philosohy.

Contents

Contents

Foreword

Aspirants often try to gain advancement in the path of spiritual ascent by following any of the specific doctrines recommended by spiritual master availed to them. They also try to follow traditions and customs which remained known to them. Alignment of human beings towards a spiritual ascent is an age old tradition. Several other religious groups developed in due course of time and a distinction between lower and higher forms of spirituality is made in between 17th and 18th Century.[1]

Spirituality became disconnected from traditional religious groups and institutions in due course of time;[2] got prominence in social and political movement of different kinds. Vedic texts and epics were translated in other languages which influenced growth of spirituality beyond the scope of religion and tradition. Role of The Bhagavadgita cannot be ignored in this regard; it was the mostly interpreted source of Holy Scriptures of Indian origin; a balanced scripture which was developed to integrate thought process of Veda, Sankhya and Yoga philosophy to elaborate possibilities and scope of spiritual ascent duly availed to aspirants from all walks of life. Spirituality was there in Asian religions in the form of secret teachings.[3] Neo- Vedanta concept and universalism of thought process was also explored during instances of global conflict to bifurcate Spirituality while remaining independent of culture and traditions dully inflicted with religion, custom and traditions.[4] Contribution of saints like Sage Shankaracharya, Swami Vivekananda, Sri Aurobindo, Acharya Vinoba and others cannot be ruled out. Advaita Vedanta was the central doctrine of the development of Spirituality during colonial rule in India. Exchange of ideas between western world and India paved a path of further development in this field for seeking subtle convergence in development of spirituality; it became more oriented on subjective experience;[5] instead of accommodating oneself in the restricted ontological context.[6] Meditation became a strong tool leading an individual to experience self actualisation.[7] Traditional doctrine encompasses spiritual progress through three distinct paths: the way of Knowledge, the way of devotion and the way of offering selfless services; there may be various combinations of all the three specified paths; even follower of all the three paths can have such eligibility.[8] Jnana Marga (the path of Knowledge) is the way of seeking self-realisation under the sincere guidance of a spiritual master

(Guru).[9] The scope of this volume of publication is to encompass development of spirituality through practices of knowledge and Science (Jnana- Vijnana). Ultimate objective of practices of Yoga is to attain renunciation of the world; a state where universal truth can be realised; where stability of memory and intellect on the Divine subject can be ensured due to diffusion of mind; where spheres of the bodily existence of the senses on worldly manifestations can be experienced as exhibits of the Divine.[10]

[1] *"Differences Between 17th Century And Early 18th Century | ipl.org". www.ipl.org. Archived from the original on 2022-11-05. Retrieved 2022-11-05.*

[2] *Snyder, C.R.; Lopez, Shane J. (2007), Positive Psychology, Sage Publications, Inc., ISBN 978-0-7619-2633-7*

[3] *McMahan, David L. (2008), The Making of Buddhist Modernism, Oxford University Press, ISBN 978-0-19-518327-6*

[4] *Roy, Sumita (2003), Aldous Huxley And Indian Thought, Sterling Publishers Pvt. Ltd*

[5] *Waaijman, Kees (2000), Spiritualiteit. Vormen, grondslagen, methoden, Kampen/Gent: Kok/Carmelitana*

[6] *Saucier, Gerard; Skrzypinska, Katarzyna (1 October 2006). "Spiritual But Not Religious? Evidence for Two Independent Dispositions" (PDF). Journal of Personality. 74 (5): 1257–92. CiteSeerX 10.1.1.548.7658. doi:10.1111/ j.1467-6494.2006.00409.x. JSTOR 27734699. PMID 16958702. Archived (PDF) from the original on 2017-08-08. Retrieved 2013-03-05.*

[7] *Houtman, Dick; Aupers, Stef (2007), "The Spiritual Turn and the Decline of Tradition: The Spread of Post-Christian Spirituality in 14 Western Countries, 1981–2000", Journal for the Scientific Study of Religion, 46 (3): 305–320, doi:10.1111/j.1468-5906.2007.00360.x*

[8] *John Lochtefeld (2002), The Illustrated Encyclopedia of Hinduism, Rosen Publishing New York, ISBN 0-8239-2287-1*

[9] *Feuerstein, Georg (2003). The deeper dimension of yoga: Theory and practice. London: Shambhala. ISBN 1-57062-935-8.*

[10] *Harung, Harald (2012). "Illustrations of Peak Experiences during Optimal Performance in World-class Performers Integrating Eastern and Western Insights". Journal of Human Values. 18 (1): 33–52. doi:10.1177/ 097168581101800104. S2CID 143106405.*

Levin, Jeff (2010). "Religion and mental health: Theory and research". International Journal of Applied Psychoanalytic Studies. 7 (2): 102–15.;

Meyer-Dinkgräfe, Daniel (2011). "Opera and spirituality". *Performance and Spirituality*. 2 (1): 38–59.

Preface

With complete attachment of mind in the Divine subject one can attain mastery in knowing real nature of the Divine Manifestations. Attainment of knowledge after gaining which nothing in this universe may remain unknown. Amongst thousands of persons, hardly one strives for gaining perfection; attainment of mastery or gain of superiority; and amongst those who have achieved such perfection, hardly any fellow aspirant knows the Divine in its real sense. Earth, water, fire, air, space, mind, intellect, and ego—these are eight components of material energy of the supreme master (or The Divine); a set of inferior energy upon which soul energy (ATMA) is the superior energy which comprises basis of the Divine manifestations. The Divine is the source of all sorts of manifestations and all such manifestations diffuse finally in the supreme source. There is nothing higher than such kind of supreme source and everything rests on such source; similar to beads remain restricted in a string; as similar as the restriction with which celestial bodies like stars continue emitting radiations; as similar to the restrictions with which stars ensure their membership to a galaxy; similar to taste of water; the sacred syllable OM (the Pranava); the sound of ether; similar to the ability in individuals; similar to the pure fragrance of the Earth, and the brilliance in fire, the life-force in all beings, the penance of the ascetics, the eternal seed of all beings, the intellect of the intelligent, the splendour of the glorious; similar to strength of individuals devoid of desires and passion; similar to the sexual activities not conflicting with virtue or scriptural injunctions. The three states of material existence[1] are manifested by the Divine while remaining ignorant about presence of such kind of supreme master; which often remains beyond the scope of access merely remaining dependent upon any of the sensible desires or mental passion. Remaining inflicted with three modes of illusions people remain ignorant of such kind of Divine omnipresence which is imperishable and eternal at all instances. [2] They also remain ignorant of the presence of such kind of doer of actions and consider themselves as the master of all such acts and conducts taken up individually by them or by imparting themselves in a group along with other performers of such action.

Aspirants who keep complete faith on the Divine will easily cross the entire world of illusions which often becomes a difficult task to accomplish by any of the common individuals remaining inflicted with complete faith on the supreme master. People who remain ignorant of knowledge, who lazily follow their lower nature of absolute knowledge, individuals inflicted with demonic nature and people having deluded intellect may not be able to recognise the Divine omnipresence. Four kinds of aspirants (the distressed, the seekers of knowledge, the seekers of worldly possessions, and those who are situated in knowledge) are capable of recognising the Divine and remain engaged in Divine subjects without deviating from the path of spiritual ascent; among these the fellow aspirant who worship the Divine will be considered as the highest; such individual gains the Divine love. Such kind of worshippers having devotion to the supreme master are indeed noble; their acts and conducts are noble; they are of steadfast mind; their intellect remains merged in the Divine subject; such individuals made the Divine alone as supreme accomplishable goal; they are considered as very self of the Divine master.[3]

Gainer of absolute knowledge having faith on the universality of the Divine is very rare in our surrounding; such knowledge always surrounds on the supreme master (BRAHMAN).[4]

A state of mental and intellectual dualities during which diffusion of knowledge becomes evident because of the mental engagements in worldly sensible desires is the condition during which aspirants rarely recognise presence of the supreme commander (BRAHMAN) in all instances of creations. Those whose knowledge has been diffused by material desires surrender to the celestial gods. Following their own nature, they worship the devatās[5], practicing rituals or meditations meant to propitiate the specified celestial personalities. [6]

Aspirants may rely on any of the godly idol or any of the masterly guide as per sincere sanction of their mind and intellect which must not generate instances of confusion or unrest;[7] for stability of mind and intellect is extremely important to enable the fellow aspirant in gaining spiritual ascent; for such kind of spiritual ascent will ensure the spiritual refinement of mind and intellect; for refined mind and intellect gradually start recognising presence of the Divine; for recognition of the Divine omnipresence will pave a path of union (Yoga) of ATMA and PARAMATMA which is the ultimate goal of life of any aspirant.

Endowed with faith, the devotee worships a particular celestial god as per development of faith in their intellect and obtains the objects of desire accordingly. Actually, the Divine alone arranges access to all sorts of benefits. Aspirants keeping faith on celestial gods get blessings accordingly and those who worship the Divine gets renunciation bit by bit.[8]

The less intelligent think that I, the Supreme Lord Shree Krishna, was formless earlier and have now assumed this personality. They do not understand the imperishable exalted nature of my personal form. The Divine is not recognisable to everyone, although without receiving such omnipresence of the supreme master nothing can be accomplished; it is because of the persistence of the illusion (YOGAMAYA); because of the prevalence of confusion in mental state; because of the shadow of ego duly inflicted with I-ness; because of the falsehood duly mounted in mind and intellect because of the attachment to passion and desire of seeking pleasure; because of vulgar nature of the mental state; because of attachment to bodily recognisable senses of pleasure; due to lack of adequate awareness of the real nature of the soul; due to sustaining faith on the illusion which remains prevalent in the immediate surroundings. That is why, those without real knowledge about the supreme master (the DIVINE) do not know that ATMA sustains without change and remains beyond the scope of birth and death.

We must acknowledge real nature of the Divine.[9] One can have freedom from all kinds of delusion.[10] Remaining involved in noble conducts one can gain freedom from development of all sorts of illusions and start recognising the real nature of the Divine manifestations at all instances.[11] One should know the principle of Karma (nature of assigned duties and performances in nature). After recognising the Divine omnipresence, striving for liberation from sequences of old-age and death, aspirants start recognising the Brahman, the individual self (ATMA), and the entire field of karmic action (KARMA).

Those who know Me as the governing principle of the adhibhūta[12] and the adhidaiva[13], and as adhiyajña[14], such enlightened souls are in full consciousness of the Divine even at the time of the disintegration of soul from the bodily manifestations.

[1] *goodness, passion, and ignorance;*
[2] *The BhagavadgitaVII. 5-13*
[3] *. (The Bhagavadgita VII.14 – 18)*
[4] *The Bhagavadgita VII. 19*
[5] *Hindi/ Sanskrit term which means the God, or the Divine; or any supreme guide having potential of taking role of a masterly guide.*
[6] *The Bhagavadgita VII.20*

[7] Whatever celestial form a devotee seeks to worship with faith, the Divine confers steadiness of that faith upon the specified form. (The Bhagavadgita VII. 21)

[8] The fruit (or result of worships) gained by aspirants alongwith little understanding is perishable. Those who worship the celestial gods move towards the celestial abodes, while devotees of the Divine finally come to the supreme master. (The Bhagavadgita VII.23)

[9] The Divine (or the supreme master) knows instances of past, present, and future, and also knows all living beings along with their true nature; but no one perfectly knows presence of the Divine at all instances.

[10] Dualities of desire and aversion arise from illusion. All living beings in the material realm are deluded by these.

[11] Aspirants, whose sins have been destroyed by engaging in pious activities, become free from the illusion of dualities; they worship the Divine (or the supreme master) with utter determination

[12] The recognisable field of matter.

[13] The entire group of celestial gods, masters and the Divine guide;

[14] the Supreme master of all sacrificial performances or YAJNA.

Acknowledgements

This volume of publication is prepared to focus on the efforts of Edwin E. Arnold, as he continued delivering his understanding of The Gita while narrating different parts of the holy scripture efficiently.

Basic understanding as arises from the study of selected parts duly taken up from the Bhagavadgita provides us a wider platform of discussion. Our attention can have affinity to correlate some of the basic instinct of individuals which often equip them to attain skills or mastery in some of the faculties; even aspirants may start moving towards attainment of absolute knowledge after attending abled guide of the Divine master.

Peace and Nonviolence can be considered as the foremost doctrine which confers the possibility of attainment of spiritual ascent in life of an aspirant. Peace is our desired level of social status and Nonviolence will be the initiative with which we want people to move on further towards the status of gaining continuation of the Peaceful resolutions in and around the state. Before considering different sources of threat to the modern society we must move through doctrines of Peace and Nonviolence along with their true nature. "Peace" is a relative term and is considered by different individuals from different view point. We can feel the peaceful situation on the basis of the mental, physical and spiritual contentment. A hungry person, for an example, cannot feel the mental and spiritual peace due to the impulse of the hunger. Similarly an individual experiencing severe pain in any of the bodily organ or system cannot experience the beauty of Meditation as some healthy person generally gains. Mahatma considered Peace as a foremost condition important for implementing Good Governance. It is also true that Peace cannot be implemented at the cost of weapons, flesh and blood; it will come through understanding of each other's need and issuing a sanction to certain extent possible for addressing wills and wishes of each other. Peace will come in its real sense for the entire community. The fulfilment of basic need of the community segments will make the initial step towards making peace process effective and result oriented. Further step will become visible in the form of regulations of need and greed of the community partners. For making our ideas more clear we should highlight different angles of consideration with which features of Truth is addressed.

We will consider distinct approaches with which "Truth" is to be addressed. True beliefs and true statements correspond to the actual state of affairs or doctrines can be considered as Truth.[1] Being a traditional model duly popularized by great thinkers and philosophers this model correlates thoughts and things in a better way. A judgement can be considered as "True" if it correlates the external reality and facts.[2] Truth is also considered as an objective reality which is often ascribed through thoughts, words and other means.[3] Obstacle due to variations of language and dialect is considered as a limiting factor due to which any universal definition of the doctrines related to "Truth (SATYA in Sanskrit) cannot be generalised. If we put concepts into practice then the result or outcome of such practice will confirm the nature of Truth (a Pragmatic Approach)[4]. Concordance of abstract statements with the ideal limit towards which hundreds of investigations can be advanced to bring out essential ingredients of Truth is considered as a basis through which one can assess Truth.[5] True is the expedient in our way of thinking and Right is the expedient in our way of behaving.[6] Truth is a quality the value of which is confirmed by the effectiveness when applying concepts into practice.

From another angle it is confirmed that what works may or may not be considered as Truth, but what fails cannot be considered as a representation of Truth. It can be advanced only because Truth never fails.[7] We cannot confer with facts and figures that we are right during all instances, but we can easily identify instances when we are wrong.[8] Nothing considered absolutely true as some other angles of observation may consider a fact true after altering the collections of facts and figures. This is a kind of superficial examination with which nature of Truth is defined. It has limitations of approach which remained restricted to the materialistic view of facts, figures, propositions and concepts. Deflationary theory maintains a clear view that "Truth" is an expressive predicate requiring no additional explanation.[9]

[1] Encyclopedia of Philosophy, Vol.2, "Correspondence Theory of Truth", auth.: Arthur N. Prior, p. 223 (Macmillan, 1969).

[2] "Correspondence Theory of Truth", in Stanford Encyclopedia of Philosophy (citing De Veritate Q.1, A.1–3 and Summa Theologiae, I. Q.16).

[3] See, e.g., Bradley, F.H., "On Truth and Copying", in Blackburn, et al. (eds., 1999),Truth, 31–45.

[4] Encyclopedia of Philosophy, Vol. 5, "Pragmatic Theory of Truth", 427 (Macmillan, 1969).

[5] *Peirce, C.S. (1901), "Truth and Falsity and Error" (in part), pp. 716–20 in James Mark Baldwin, ed., Dictionary of Philosophy and Psychology, v. 2. Peirce's section is entitled "Logical", beginning on p. 718, column 1, and ending on p. 720 with the initials "(C.S.P.)"*

[6] *James, William, The Meaning of Truth, A Sequel to 'Pragmatism', (1909).*

[7] *Sahakian, W.S. & Sahakian, M.L., Ideas of the Great Philosophers, New York: Barnes & Noble, 1966, LCCN 66--23155*

[8] *Feynman, The Character of Physical Law, New York: Random House, 1994, ISBN 0-679-60127-9.*

[9] *Encyclopedia of Philosophy, Supp., "Truth", auth: Michael Williams, pp. 572–73 (Macmillan, 1996)*

Prologue

Practice of Nonviolence is strategic or pragmatic.[5] Our in-capabilities of distinguishing these two types of approaches may lead towards development of confusion.[6] Both types of nonviolent approaches finally move on with distinct goals, philosophies and spiritual alignments in particular.[7] Nonviolent approaches reject the use of violent operations for bringing justice for people. It also encompasses acceptance of some alternative path (popularly termed as Passive resistance) for making people aware of their rights and duties. If justice is considered as a birth right then one could claim such right in a society by adjusting their aspirations with positive waves of participation impregnated with efforts of exercising a structured claim on such rights without raising weapons.[8] Nonviolent movements also remain progressive in society without bringing any kind of fear in the minds of any of the partners of movement. It also ensures adequate spiritual and intellectual alignment of the individuals taking part in the system of guided movement.[9] Movement duly planned in accord to the model of Passive Resistance may continue for a longer time, but it will bring assured success without developing any kind of hatred or casualties on either side. This approach of addressing features of nonviolence ensures the linkage of nonviolence with peace.[10] Both peace and nonviolence is a pair of wheels upon which the chariot of personality is established. Simply absence of violence cannot characterize the feature of nonviolence (AHIMSA) is a better way. To trace out the real nature of the doctrine of Nonviolence we have to move back through pages of scriptures and Epics. Yoga Philosophy defined the ritual of Nonviolence in such a way that highest spiritual refinement of an individual is duly accommodated in that ritual. It defines Nonviolence (AHIMSA) as follows:

"If we say that Nonviolence (AHIMSA) is established in any context then organisms residing that context will coexist with family feelings. They even cast off their feelings of hatred and agony. They make them contented by exercising living within minimum."

If we try to restrict this doctrine of Peace and Nonviolence then also it will become evident that both nonviolence and peace got adequate importance in all schools of religion. None of the religions in this world preaches people to adopt violent means for ensuring survival and prosperity of community members. Ethical philosophy of Jainism (after Saint

Mahaveera) prepared an extraordinary status for the doctrine of Peace and Nonviolence.[11] Attentiveness of the law making and law implementing agencies ensure chances of acceptance or rejection of nonviolent proposals during any of the instances as per need or as per consent of people.[12]

[1] *Paul F. Robinson (2003), Just War in Comparative Perspective, ISBN 0-7546-3587-2, Ashgate Publishing, see pages 114–125*

[2] *Subedi, S. P. (2003). The Concept in Hinduism of 'Just War'. Journal of Conflict and Security Law, 8(2), pages 339–361*

[3] *Subedi, S. P. (2003). The Concept in Hinduism of 'Just War'. Journal of Conflict and Security Law, 8(2), pages 339–361*

[4] *Ueshiba, Kisshōmaru (2004), The Art of Aikido: Principles and Essential Techniques, Kodansha International, ISBN 4-7700-2945-4*

[5] *A clarification of this and related terms appears in Gene Sharp, Sharp's Dictionary of Power and Struggle: Language of Civil Resistance in Conflicts, Oxford University Press, New York, 2012.*

[6] *Weber, Thomas (2003). "Nonviolence is who? Gene sharp and Gandhi". Peace & Change. 28 (2): 250.*

[7] *Nepstad, Sharon Erickson (2015). Nonviolent struggle : theories, strategies, and dynamics. New York. ISBN 978-0-19-997599-0. OCLC 903248163.*

[8] *"James L. Bevel The Strategist of the 1960s Civil Rights Movement" by Randall L. Kryn, a paper in David Garrow's 1989 book We Shall Overcome Volume II, Carlson Publishing Company*

[9] *Ives, Susan (19 October 2001). "No Fear". Palo Alto College. Archived from the original on 20 July 2008. Retrieved 2009-05-17.*

[10] *Ackerman, Peter and Jack DuVall (2001) A Force More Powerful: A Century of Non-Violent Conflict (Palgrave Macmillan)*

[11] *Stephen H. Phillips & other authors (2008), in Encyclopedia of Violence, Peace, & Conflict (Second Edition), ISBN 978-0-12-373985-8, Elsevier Science, Pages 1347–1356, 701–849, 1867.*

[12] *Sharp, Gene (1973). The Politics of Nonviolent Action. Porter Sargent. p. 12. ISBN 978-0-87558-068-5.*

Chapter One

Dhritirashtra:
   Ranged thus for battle on the sacred plain--
   On Kurukshetra--say, Sanjaya! say
   What wrought my people, and the Pandavas?
Sanjaya:
   When he beheld the host of Pandavas,
   Raja Duryodhana to Drona drew,
   And spake these words: "Ah, Guru! see this line,
   How vast it is of Pandu fighting-men,
   Embattled by the son of Drupada,
   Thy scholar in the war! Therein stand ranked
   Chiefs like Arjuna, like to Bhima chiefs,
   Benders of bows; Virata, Yuyudhan,
   Drupada, eminent upon his car,
   Dhrishtaket, Chekitan, Kasi's stout lord,
   Purujit, Kuntibhoj, and Saivya,
   With Yudhamanyu, and Uttamauj
   Subhadra's child; and Drupadi's;-all famed!
   All mounted on their shining chariots!
   On our side, too,--thou best of Brahmans! see
   Excellent chiefs, commanders of my line,
   Whose names I joy to count: thyself the first,
   Then Bhishma, Karna, Kripa fierce in fight,
   Vikarna, Aswatthaman; next to these
   Strong Saumadatti, with full many more
   Valiant and tried, ready this day to die
   For me their king, each with his weapon grasped,
   Each skilful in the field. Weakest-meseems-

Our battle shows where Bhishma holds command,
And Bhima, fronting him, something too strong!
Have care our captains nigh to Bhishma's ranks
Prepare what help they may! Now, blow my shell!"
Then, at the signal of the aged king,
With blare to wake the blood, rolling around
Like to a lion's roar, the trumpeter
Blew the great Conch; and, at the noise of it,
Trumpets and drums, cymbals and gongs and horns
Burst into sudden clamour; as the blasts
Of loosened tempest, such the tumult seemed!
Then might be seen, upon their car of gold
Yoked with white steeds, blowing their battle-shells,
Krishna the God, Arjuna at his side:
Krishna, with knotted locks, blew his great conch
Carved of the "Giant's bone;" Arjuna blew
Indra's loud gift; Bhima the terrible--
Wolf-bellied Bhima-blew a long reed-conch;
And Yudhisthira, Kunti's blameless son,
Winded a mighty shell, "Victory's Voice;"
And Nakula blew shrill upon his conch
Named the "Sweet-sounding," Sahadev on his
Called"Gem-bedecked," and Kasi's Prince on his.
Sikhandi on his car, Dhrishtadyumn,
Virata, Satyaki the Unsubdued,
Drupada, with his sons, (O Lord of Earth!)
Long-armed Subhadra's children, all blew loud,
So that the clangour shook their foemen's hearts,
With quaking earth and thundering heav'n.
Then 'twas-
Beholding Dhritirashtra's battle set,
Weapons unsheathing, bows drawn forth, the war
Instant to break-Arjun, whose ensign-badge
Was Hanuman the monkey, spake this thing
To Krishna the Divine, his charioteer:
"Drive, Dauntless One! to yonder open ground
Betwixt the armies; I would see more nigh
These who will fight with us, those we must slay

To-day, in war's arbitrament; for, sure,
On bloodshed all are bent who throng this plain,
Obeying Dhritirashtra's sinful son."
Thus, by Arjuna prayed, (O Bharata!)
Between the hosts that heavenly Charioteer
Drove the bright car, reining its milk-white steeds
Where Bhishma led, and Drona,and their Lords.
"See!" spake he to Arjuna, "where they stand,
Thy kindred of the Kurus:" and the Prince
Marked on each hand the kinsmen of his house,
Grandsires and sires, uncles and brothers and sons,
Cousins and sons-in-law and nephews, mixed
With friends and honoured elders; some this side,
Some that side ranged: and, seeing those opposed,
Such kith grown enemies-Arjuna's heart
Melted with pity, while he uttered this:
Arjuna.
Krishna! as I behold, come here to shed
Their common blood, yon concourse of our kin,
My members fail, my tongue dries in my mouth,
A shudder thrills my body, and my hair
Bristles with horror; from my weak hand slips
Gandiv, the goodly bow; a fever burns
My skin to parching; hardly may I stand;
The life within me seems to swim and faint;
Nothing do I foresee save woe and wail!
It is not good, O Keshav! nought of good
Can spring from mutual slaughter! Lo, I hate
Triumph and domination, wealth and ease,
Thus sadly won! Aho! what victory
Can bring delight, Govinda! what rich spoils
Could profit; what rule recompense; what span
Of life itself seem sweet, bought with such blood?
Seeing that these stand here, ready to die,
For whose sake life was fair, and pleasure pleased,
And power grew precious:-grandsires, sires, and sons,
Brothers, and fathers-in-law, and sons-in-law,
Elders and friends! Shall I deal death on these

Even though they seek to slay us? Not one blow,
O Madhusudan! will I strike to gain
The rule of all Three Worlds; then, how much less
To seize an earthly kingdom! Killing these
Must breed but anguish, Krishna! If they be
Guilty, we shall grow guilty by their deaths;
Their sins will light on us, if we shall slay
Those sons of Dhritirashtra, and our kin;
What peace could come of that, O Madhava?
For if indeed, blinded by lust and wrath,
These cannot see, or will not see, the sin
Of kingly lines o'erthrown and kinsmen slain,
How should not we, who see, shun such a crime--
We who perceive the guilt and feel the shame--
O thou Delight of Men, Janardana?
By overthrow of houses perisheth
Their sweet continuous household piety,
And-rites neglected, piety extinct--
Enters impiety upon that home;
Its women grow unwomaned, whence there spring
Mad passions, and the mingling-up of castes,
Sending a Hell-ward road that family,
And whoso wrought its doom by wicked wrath.
Nay, and the souls of honoured ancestors
Fall from their place of peace, being bereft
Of funeral-cakes and the wan death-water.[1]
So teach our holy hymns. Thus, if we slay
Kinsfolk and friends for love of earthly power,
Ahovat! what an evil fault it were!
Better I deem it, if my kinsmen strike,
To face them weaponless, and bare my breast
To shaft and spear, than answer blow with blow.
So speaking, in the face of those two hosts,
Arjuna sank upon his chariot-seat,
And let fall bow and arrows, sick at heart.
HERE ENDETH CHAPTER I. OF THE BHAGAVAD-GITA,
Entitled "Arjun-Vishad,"
Or "The Book of the Distress of Arjuna."

[1] *Some repetitionary lines are here omitted.*

CHAPTER TWO

Two

Sanjaya.
    Him, filled with such compassion and such grief,
    With eyes tear-dimmed, despondent, in stern words
    The Driver, Madhusudan, thus addressed:
    Krishna.
    How hath this weakness taken thee? Whence springs
    The inglorious trouble, shameful to the brave,
    Barring the path of virtue? Nay, Arjun!
    Forbid thyself to feebleness! it mars
    Thy warrior-name! cast off the coward-fit!
    Wake! Be thyself! Arise, Scourge of thy Foes!
    Arjuna.
    How can I, in the battle, shoot with shafts
    On Bhishma, or on Drona-O thou Chief!--
    Both worshipful, both honourable men?
    Better to live on beggar's bread
    With those we love alive,
    Than taste their blood in rich feasts spread,
    And guiltily survive!
    Ah! were it worse-who knows?--to be
    Victor or vanquished here,
    When those confront us angrily
    Whose death leaves living drear?
    In pity lost, by doubtings tossed,
    My thoughts-distracted-turn
    To Thee, the Guide I reverence most,
    That I may counsel learn:
    I know not what would heal the grief

Burned into soul and sense,
If I were earth's unchallenged chief--
A god--and these gone thence!
Sanjaya.
So spake Arjuna to the Lord of Hearts,
And sighing,"I will not fight!" held silence then.
To whom, with tender smile, (O Bharata!)
While the Prince wept despairing 'twixt those hosts,
Krishna made answer in divinest verse:
Krishna.
Thou grievest where no grief should be! thou speak'st
Words lacking wisdom! for the wise in heart
Mourn not for those that live, nor those that die.
Nor I, nor thou, nor any one of these,
Ever was not, nor ever will not be,
For ever and for ever afterwards.
All, that doth live, lives always! To man's frame
As there come infancy and youth and age,
So come there raisings-up and layings-down
Of other and of other life-abodes,
Which the wise know, and fear not. This that irks--
Thy sense-life, thrilling to the elements--
Bringing thee heat and cold, sorrows and joys,
'Tis brief and mutable! Bear with it, Prince!
As the wise bear. The soul which is not moved,
The soul that with a strong and constant calm
Takes sorrow and takes joy indifferently,
Lives in the life undying! That which is
Can never cease to be; that which is not
Will not exist. To see this truth of both
Is theirs who part essence from accident,
Substance from shadow. Indestructible,
Learn thou! the Life is, spreading life through all;
It cannot anywhere, by any means,
Be anywise diminished, stayed, or changed.
But for these fleeting frames which it informs
With spirit deathless, endless, infinite,
They perish. Let them perish, Prince! and fight!

He who shall say, "Lo! I have slain a man!"
He who shall think, "Lo! I am slain!" those both
Know naught! Life cannot slay. Life is not slain!
Never the spirit was born; the spirit shall cease to be never;
Never was time it was not; End and Beginning are dreams!
Birthless and deathless and changeless remaineth the spirit for ever;
Death hath not touched it at all, dead though the house of it seems!
Who knoweth it exhaustless, self-sustained,
Immortal, indestructible,--shall such
Say, "I have killed a man, or caused to kill?"
Nay, but as when one layeth
His worn-out robes away,
And taking new ones, sayeth,
"These will I wear to-day!"
So putteth by the spirit
Lightly its garb of flesh,
And passeth to inherit
A residence afresh.
I say to thee weapons reach not the Life;
Flame burns it not, waters cannot o'erwhelm,
Nor dry winds wither it. Impenetrable,
Unentered, unassailed, unharmed, untouched,
Immortal, all-arriving, stable, sure,
Invisible, ineffable, by word
And thought uncompassed, ever all itself,
Thus is the Soul declared! How wilt thou, then,--
Knowing it so,--grieve when thou shouldst not grieve?
How, if thou hearest that the man new-dead
Is, like the man new-born, still living man--
One same, existent Spirit--wilt thou weep?
The end of birth is death; the end of death
Is birth: this is ordained! and mournest thou,
Chief of the stalwart arm! for what befalls
Which could not otherwise befall? The birth
Of living things comes unperceived; the death
Comes unperceived; between them, beings perceive:
What is there sorrowful herein, dear Prince?
Wonderful, wistful, to contemplate!

Difficult, doubtful, to speak upon!
Strange and great for tongue to relate,
Mystical hearing for every one!
Nor wotteth man this, what a marvel it is,
When seeing, and saying, and hearing are done!
This Life within all living things, my Prince!
Hides beyond harm; scorn thou to suffer, then,
For that which cannot suffer. Do thy part!
Be mindful of thy name, and tremble not!
Nought better can betide a martial soul
Than lawful war; happy the warrior
To whom comes joy of battle--comes, as now,
Glorious and fair, unsought; opening for him
A gateway unto Heav'n. But, if thou shunn'st
This honourable field--a Kshattriya--
If, knowing thy duty and thy task, thou bidd'st
Duty and task go by--that shall be sin!
And those to come shall speak thee infamy
From age to age; but infamy is worse
For men of noble blood to bear than death!
The chiefs upon their battle-chariots
Will deem 'twas fear that drove thee from the fray.
Of those who held thee mighty-souled the scorn
Thou must abide, while all thine enemies
Will scatter bitter speech of thee, to mock
The valour which thou hadst; what fate could fall
More grievously than this? Either--being killed--
Thou wilt win Swarga's safety, or--alive
And victor--thou wilt reign an earthly king.
Therefore, arise, thou Son of Kunti! brace
Thine arm for conflict, nerve thy heart to meet--
As things alike to thee--pleasure or pain,
Profit or ruin, victory or defeat:
So minded, gird thee to the fight, for so
Thou shalt not sin!
Thus far I speak to thee
As from the "Sankhya"--unspiritually--
Hear now the deeper teaching of the Yog,

Which holding, understanding, thou shalt burst
Thy Karmabandh, the bondage of wrought deeds.
Here shall no end be hindered, no hope marred,
No loss be feared: faith--yea, a little faith--
Shall save thee from the anguish of thy dread.
Here, Glory of the Kurus! shines one rule--
One steadfast rule--while shifting souls have laws
Many and hard. Specious, but wrongful deem
The speech of those ill-taught ones who extol
The letter of their Vedas, saying, "This
Is all we have, or need;" being weak at heart
With wants, seekers of Heaven: which comes--they say--
As "fruit of good deeds done;" promising men
Much profit in new births for works of faith;
In various rites abounding; following whereon
Large merit shall accrue towards wealth and power;
Albeit, who wealth and power do most desire
Least fixity of soul have such, least hold
On heavenly meditation. Much these teach,
From Veds, concerning the "three qualities;"
But thou, be free of the "three qualities,"
Free of the "pairs of opposites,"[1] and free
From that sad righteousness which calculates;
Self-ruled, Arjuna! simple, satisfied![2]
Look! like as when a tank pours water forth
To suit all needs, so do these Brahmans draw
Text for all wants from tank of Holy Writ.
But thou, want not! ask not! Find full reward
Of doing right in right! Let right deeds be
Thy motive, not the fruit which comes from them.
And live in action! Labour! Make thine acts
Thy piety, casting all self aside,
Contemning gain and merit; equable
In good or evil: equability
Is Yog, is piety!
Yet, the right act
Is less, far less, than the right-thinking mind.
Seek refuge in thy soul; have there thy heaven!

Scorn them that follow virtue for her gifts!
The mind of pure devotion--even here--
Casts equally aside good deeds and bad,
Passing above them. Unto pure devotion
Devote thyself: with perfect meditation
Comes perfect act, and the right-hearted rise--
More certainly because they seek no gain--
Forth from the bands of body, step by step,
To highest seats of bliss. When thy firm soul
Hath shaken off those tangled oracles
Which ignorantly guide, then shall it soar
To high neglect of what's denied or said,
This way or that way, in doctrinal writ.
Troubled no longer by the priestly lore,
Safe shall it live, and sure; steadfastly bent
On meditation. This is Yog--and Peace!
Arjuna.
What is his mark who hath that steadfast heart,
Confirmed in holy meditation? How
Know we his speech, Kesava? Sits he, moves he
Like other men?
Krishna.
When one, O Pritha's Son!
Abandoning desires which shake the mind--
Finds in his soul full comfort for his soul,
He hath attained the Yog--that man is such!
In sorrows not dejected, and in joys
Not overjoyed; dwelling outside the stress
Of passion, fear, and anger; fixed in calms
Of lofty contemplation;--such an one
Is Muni, is the Sage, the true Recluse!
He who to none and nowhere overbound
By ties of flesh, takes evil things and good
Neither desponding nor exulting, such
Bears wisdom's plainest mark! He who shall draw
As the wise tortoise draws its four feet safe
Under its shield, his five frail senses back
Under the spirit's buckler from the world

Which else assails them, such an one, my Prince!
Hath wisdom's mark! Things that solicit sense
Hold off from the self-governed; nay, it comes,
The appetites of him who lives beyond
Depart,--aroused no more. Yet may it chance,
O Son of Kunti! that a governed mind
Shall some time feel the sense-storms sweep, and wrest
Strong self-control by the roots. Let him regain
His kingdom! let him conquer this, and sit
On Me intent. That man alone is wise
Who keeps the mastery of himself! If one
Ponders on objects of the sense, there springs
Attraction; from attraction grows desire,
Desire flames to fierce passion, passion breeds
Recklessness; then the memory--all betrayed--
Lets noble purpose go, and saps the mind,
Till purpose, mind, and man are all undone.
But, if one deals with objects of the sense
Not loving and not hating, making them
Serve his free soul, which rests serenely lord,
Lo! such a man comes to tranquillity;
And out of that tranquillity shall rise
The end and healing of his earthly pains,
Since the will governed sets the soul at peace.
The soul of the ungoverned is not his,
Nor hath he knowledge of himself; which lacked,
How grows serenity? and, wanting that,
Whence shall he hope for happiness?

Description: I:\Geetai-Mission-2022\Edwin Arnold\1.jpg

The mind
That gives itself to follow shows of sense
Seeth its helm of wisdom rent away,
And, like a ship in waves of whirlwind, drives
To wreck and death. Only with him, great Prince!
Whose senses are not swayed by things of sense--
Only with him who holds his mastery,
Shows wisdom perfect. What is midnight-gloom
To unenlightened souls shines wakeful day
To his clear gaze; what seems as wakeful day
Is known for night, thick night of ignorance,
To his true-seeing eyes. Such is the Saint!
And like the ocean, day by day receiving
Floods from all lands, which never overflows
Its boundary-line not leaping, and not leaving,
Fed by the rivers, but unswelled by those;--
So is the perfect one! to his soul's ocean
The world of sense pours streams of witchery;
They leave him as they find, without commotion,
Taking their tribute, but remaining sea.
Yea! whoso, shaking off the yoke of flesh
Lives lord, not servant, of his lusts; set free
From pride, from passion, from the sin of "Self,"
Toucheth tranquillity! O Pritha's Son!
That is the state of Brahm! There rests no dread
When that last step is reached! Live where he will,

Die when he may, such passeth from all 'plaining,
To blest Nirvana, with the Gods, attaining.
HERE ENDETH CHAPTER II. OF THE BHAGAVAD-GITA,
Entitled "Sankhya-Yog,"
Or "The Book of Doctrines."
[1] Technical phrases of Vedic religion.
[2] The whole of this passage is highly involved and difficult to render.

Three

Arjuna.

    Thou whom all mortals praise, Janardana!
If meditation be a nobler thing
Than action, wherefore, then, great Kesava!
Dost thou impel me to this dreadful fight?
Now am I by thy doubtful speech disturbed!
Tell me one thing, and tell me certainly;
By what road shall I find the better end?

Krishna.

I told thee, blameless Lord! there be two paths
Shown to this world; two schools of wisdom. First
The Sankhya's, which doth save in way of works
Prescribed[1] by reason; next, the Yog, which bids
Attain by meditation, spiritually:
Yet these are one! No man shall 'scape from act
By shunning action; nay, and none shall come
By mere renouncements unto perfectness.
Nay, and no jot of time, at any time,
Rests any actionless; his nature's law
Compels him, even unwilling, into act;
[For thought is act in fancy]. He who sits
Suppressing all the instruments of flesh,
Yet in his idle heart thinking on them,
Plays the inept and guilty hypocrite:
But he who, with strong body serving mind,
Gives up his mortal powers to worthy work,
Not seeking gain, Arjuna! such an one

Is honourable. Do thine allotted task!
Work is more excellent than idleness;
The body's life proceeds not, lacking work.
There is a task of holiness to do,
Unlike world-binding toil, which bindeth not
The faithful soul; such earthly duty do
Free from desire, and thou shalt well perform
Thy heavenly purpose. Spake Prajapati--
In the beginning, when all men were made,
And, with mankind, the sacrifice-- "Do this!
Work! sacrifice! Increase and multiply
With sacrifice! This shall be Kamaduk,
Your 'Cow of Plenty,' giving back her milk
Of all abundance. Worship the gods thereby;
The gods shall yield thee grace. Those meats ye crave
The gods will grant to Labour, when it pays
Tithes in the altar-flame. But if one eats
Fruits of the earth, rendering to kindly Heaven
No gift of toil, that thief steals from his world."
Who eat of food after their sacrifice
Are quit of fault, but they that spread a feast
All for themselves, eat sin and drink of sin.
By food the living live; food comes of rain,
And rain comes by the pious sacrifice,
And sacrifice is paid with tithes of toil;
Thus action is of Brahma, who is One,
The Only, All-pervading; at all times
Present in sacrifice. He that abstains
To help the rolling wheels of this great world,
Glutting his idle sense, lives a lost life,
Shameful and vain. Existing for himself,
Self-concentrated, serving self alone,
No part hath he in aught; nothing achieved,
Nought wrought or unwrought toucheth him; no hope
Of help for all the living things of earth
Depends from him.[2] Therefore, thy task prescribed
With spirit unattached gladly perform,
Since in performance of plain duty man

Mounts to his highest bliss. By works alone
Janak and ancient saints reached blessedness!
Moreover, for the upholding of thy kind,
Action thou should'st embrace. What the wise choose
The unwise people take; what best men do
The multitude will follow. Look on me,
Thou Son of Pritha! in the three wide worlds
I am not bound to any toil, no height
Awaits to scale, no gift remains to gain,
Yet I act here! and, if I acted not--
Earnest and watchful--those that look to me
For guidance, sinking back to sloth again
Because I slumbered, would decline from good,
And I should break earth's order and commit
Her offspring unto ruin, Bharata!
Even as the unknowing toil, wedded to sense,
So let the enlightened toil, sense-freed, but set
To bring the world deliverance, and its bliss;
Not sowing in those simple, busy hearts
Seed of despair. Yea! let each play his part
In all he finds to do, with unyoked soul.
All things are everywhere by Nature wrought
In interaction of the qualities.
The fool, cheated by self, thinks, "This I did"
And "That I wrought; "but--ah, thou strong-armed Prince!--
A better-lessoned mind, knowing the play
Of visible things within the world of sense,
And how the qualities must qualify,
Standeth aloof even from his acts. Th' untaught
Live mixed with them, knowing not Nature's way,
Of highest aims unwitting, slow and dull.
Those make thou not to stumble, having the light;
But all thy dues discharging, for My sake,
With meditation centred inwardly,
Seeking no profit, satisfied, serene,
Heedless of issue--fight! They who shall keep
My ordinance thus, the wise and willing hearts,
Have quittance from all issue of their acts;

But those who disregard My ordinance,
Thinking they know, know nought, and fall to loss,
Confused and foolish. 'Sooth, the instructed one
Doth of his kind, following what fits him most:
And lower creatures of their kind; in vain
Contending 'gainst the law. Needs must it be
The objects of the sense will stir the sense
To like and dislike, yet th' enlightened man
Yields not to these, knowing them enemies.
Finally, this is better, that one do
His own task as he may, even though he fail,
Than take tasks not his own, though they seem good.
To die performing duty is no ill;
But who seeks other roads shall wander still.
Arjuna.
Yet tell me, Teacher! by what force doth man
Go to his ill, unwilling; as if one
Pushed him that evil path?
Krishna.
Kama it is!
Passion it is! born of the Darknesses,
Which pusheth him. Mighty of appetite,
Sinful, and strong is this!--man's enemy!
As smoke blots the white fire, as clinging rust
Mars the bright mirror, as the womb surrounds
The babe unborn, so is the world of things
Foiled, soiled, enclosed in this desire of flesh.
The wise fall, caught in it; the unresting foe
It is of wisdom, wearing countless forms,
Fair but deceitful, subtle as a flame.
Sense, mind, and reason--these, O Kunti's Son!
Are booty for it; in its play with these
It maddens man, beguiling, blinding him.
Therefore, thou noblest child of Bharata!
Govern thy heart! Constrain th' entangled sense!
Resist the false, soft sinfulness which saps
Knowledge and judgment! Yea, the world is strong,
But what discerns it stronger, and the mind

Strongest; and high o'er all the ruling Soul.
Wherefore, perceiving Him who reigns supreme,
Put forth full force of Soul in thy own soul!
Fight! vanquish foes and doubts, dear Hero! slay
What haunts thee in fond shapes, and would betray!
HERE ENDETH CHAPTER III. OF THE BHAGAVAD-GITA,
Entitled "Karma-Yog,"
Or "The Book of Virtue in Work."
[1] I feel convinced sankhyanan and yoginan must be transposed here in sense.

[2] *I am doubtful of accuracy here.*

Four

Krishna.

This deathless Yoga, this deep union,
I taught Vivaswata,[1] the Lord of Light;
Vivaswata to Manu gave it; he
To Ikshwaku; so passed it down the line
Of all my royal Rishis. Then, with years,
The truth grew dim and perished, noble Prince!
Now once again to thee it is declared--
This ancient lore, this mystery supreme--
Seeing I find thee votary and friend.
Arjuna.

Thy birth, dear Lord, was in these later days,
And bright Vivaswata's preceded time!
How shall I comprehend this thing thou sayest,
"From the beginning it was I who taught?"
Krishna.

Manifold the renewals of my birth
Have been, Arjuna! and of thy births, too!
But mine I know, and thine thou knowest not,
O Slayer of thy Foes! Albeit I be
Unborn, undying, indestructible,
The Lord of all things living; not the less--
By Maya, by my magic which I stamp
On floating Nature-forms, the primal vast--
I come, and go, and come. When Righteousness
Declines, O Bharata! when Wickedness
Is strong, I rise, from age to age, and take
Visible shape, and move a man with men,

Succouring the good, thrusting the evil back,
And setting Virtue on her seat again.
Who knows the truth touching my births on earth
And my divine work, when he quits the flesh
Puts on its load no more, falls no more down
To earthly birth: to Me he comes, dear Prince!
Many there be who come! from fear set free,
From anger, from desire; keeping their hearts
Fixed upon me--my Faithful--purified
By sacred flame of Knowledge. Such as these
Mix with my being. Whoso worship me,
Them I exalt; but all men everywhere
Shall fall into my path; albeit, those souls
Which seek reward for works, make sacrifice
Now, to the lower gods. I say to thee
Here have they their reward. But I am He
Made the Four Castes, and portioned them a place
After their qualities and gifts. Yea, I
Created, the Reposeful; I that live
Immortally, made all those mortal births:
For works soil not my essence, being works
Wrought uninvolved.[2] Who knows me acting thus
Unchained by action, action binds not him;
And, so perceiving, all those saints of old
Worked, seeking for deliverance. Work thou
As, in the days gone by, thy fathers did.
Thou sayst, perplexed, It hath been asked before
By singers and by sages, "What is act,
And what inaction? "I will teach thee this,
And, knowing, thou shalt learn which work doth save
Needs must one rightly meditate those three--
Doing,--not doing,--and undoing. Here
Thorny and dark the path is! He who sees
How action may be rest, rest action--he
Is wisest 'mid his kind; he hath the truth!
He doeth well, acting or resting. Freed
In all his works from prickings of desire,
Burned clean in act by the white fire of truth,

The wise call that man wise; and such an one,
Renouncing fruit of deeds, always content.
Always self-satisfying, if he works,
Doth nothing that shall stain his separate soul,
Which--quit of fear and hope--subduing self--
Rejecting outward impulse--yielding up
To body's need nothing save body, dwells
Sinless amid all sin, with equal calm
Taking what may befall, by grief unmoved,
Unmoved by joy, unenvyingly; the same
In good and evil fortunes; nowise bound
By bond of deeds. Nay, but of such an one,
Whose crave is gone, whose soul is liberate,
Whose heart is set on truth--of such an one
What work he does is work of sacrifice,
Which passeth purely into ash and smoke
Consumed upon the altar! All's then God!
The sacrifice is Brahm, the ghee and grain
Are Brahm, the fire is Brahm, the flesh it eats
Is Brahm, and unto Brahm attaineth he
Who, in such office, meditates on Brahm.
Some votaries there be who serve the gods
With flesh and altar-smoke; but other some
Who, lighting subtler fires, make purer rite
With will of worship. Of the which be they
Who, in white flame of continence, consume
Joys of the sense, delights of eye and ear,
Forgoing tender speech and sound of song:
And they who, kindling fires with torch of Truth,
Burn on a hidden altar-stone the bliss
Of youth and love, renouncing happiness:
And they who lay for offering there their wealth,
Their penance, meditation, piety,
Their steadfast reading of the scrolls, their lore
Painfully gained with long austerities:
And they who, making silent sacrifice,
Draw in their breath to feed the flame of thought,
And breathe it forth to waft the heart on high,

Governing the ventage of each entering air
Lest one sigh pass which helpeth not the soul:
And they who, day by day denying needs,
Lay life itself upon the altar-flame,
Burning the body wan. Lo! all these keep
The rite of offering, as if they slew
Victims; and all thereby efface much sin.
Yea! and who feed on the immortal food
Left of such sacrifice, to Brahma pass,
To The Unending. But for him that makes
No sacrifice, he hath nor part nor lot
Even in the present world. How should he share
Another, O thou Glory of thy Line?
In sight of Brahma all these offerings
Are spread and are accepted! Comprehend
That all proceed by act; for knowing this,
Thou shalt be quit of doubt. The sacrifice
Which Knowledge pays is better than great gifts
Offered by wealth, since gifts' worth--O my Prince!
Lies in the mind which gives, the will that serves:
And these are gained by reverence, by strong search,
By humble heed of those who see the Truth
And teach it. Knowing Truth, thy heart no more
Will ache with error, for the Truth shall show
All things subdued to thee, as thou to Me.
Moreover, Son of Pandu! wert thou worst
Of all wrong-doers, this fair ship of Truth
Should bear thee safe and dry across the sea
Of thy transgressions. As the kindled flame
Feeds on the fuel till it sinks to ash,
So unto ash, Arjuna! unto nought
The flame of Knowledge wastes works' dross away!
There is no purifier like thereto
In all this world, and he who seeketh it
Shall find it--being grown perfect--in himself.
Believing, he receives it when the soul
Masters itself, and cleaves to Truth, and comes--
Possessing knowledge--to the higher peace,

The uttermost repose. But those untaught,
And those without full faith, and those who fear
Are shent; no peace is here or other where,
No hope, nor happiness for whoso doubts.
He that, being self-contained, hath vanquished doubt,
Disparting self from service, soul from works,
Enlightened and emancipate, my Prince!
Works fetter him no more! Cut then atwain
With sword of wisdom, Son of Bharata!
This doubt that binds thy heart-beats! cleave the bond
Born of thy ignorance! Be bold and wise!
Give thyself to the field with me! Arise!
HERE ENDETH CHAPTER IV. OF THE BHAGAVAD-GITA,
Entitled "Jnana Yog,"
Or "The Book of the Religion of Knowledge,"
[1] *A name of the sun.*
[2] *Without desire of fruit.*

Five

Arjuna.

Yet, Krishna! at the one time thou dost laud
Surcease of works, and, at another time,
Service through work. Of these twain plainly tell
Which is the better way?
Krishna.
To cease from works
Is well, and to do works in holiness
Is well; and both conduct to bliss supreme;
But of these twain the better way is his
Who working piously refraineth not.
That is the true Renouncer, firm and fixed,
Who--seeking nought, rejecting nought--dwells proof
Against the "opposites."[1] O valiant Prince!
In doing, such breaks lightly from all deed:
'Tis the new scholar talks as they were two,
This Sankhya and this Yoga: wise men know
Who husbands one plucks golden fruit of both!
The region of high rest which Sankhyans reach
Yogins attain. Who sees these twain as one
Sees with clear eyes! Yet such abstraction, Chief!
Is hard to win without much holiness.
Whoso is fixed in holiness, self-ruled,
Pure-hearted, lord of senses and of self,
Lost in the common life of all which lives--
A "Yogayukt"--he is a Saint who wends
Straightway to Brahm. Such an one is not touched
By taint of deeds. "Nought of myself I do!"

Thus will he think-who holds the truth of truths--
In seeing, hearing, touching, smelling; when
He eats, or goes, or breathes; slumbers or talks,
Holds fast or loosens, opes his eyes or shuts;
Always assured "This is the sense-world plays
With senses."He that acts in thought of Brahm,
Detaching end from act, with act content,
The world of sense can no more stain his soul
Than waters mar th' enamelled lotus-leaf.
With life, with heart, with mind,-nay, with the help
Of all five senses--letting selfhood go--
Yogins toil ever towards their souls' release.
Such votaries, renouncing fruit of deeds,
Gain endless peace: the unvowed, the passion-bound,
Seeking a fruit from works, are fastened down.
The embodied sage, withdrawn within his soul,
At every act sits godlike in "the town
Which hath nine gateways,"[2] neither doing aught
Nor causing any deed. This world's Lord makes
Neither the work, nor passion for the work,
Nor lust for fruit of work; the man's own self
Pushes to these! The Master of this World
Takes on himself the good or evil deeds
Of no man--dwelling beyond! Mankind errs here
By folly, darkening knowledge. But, for whom
That darkness of the soul is chased by light,
Splendid and clear shines manifest the Truth
As if a Sun of Wisdom sprang to shed
Its beams of dawn. Him meditating still,
Him seeking, with Him blended, stayed on Him,
The souls illuminated take that road
Which hath no turning back--their sins flung off
By strength of faith. [Who will may have this Light;
Who hath it sees.] To him who wisely sees,
The Brahman with his scrolls and sanctities,
The cow, the elephant, the unclean dog,
The Outcast gorging dog's meat, are all one.
The world is overcome--aye! even here!

By such as fix their faith on Unity.
The sinless Brahma dwells in Unity,
And they in Brahma. Be not over-glad
Attaining joy, and be not over-sad
Encountering grief, but, stayed on Brahma, still
Constant let each abide! The sage whose soul
Holds off from outer contacts, in himself
Finds bliss; to Brahma joined by piety,
His spirit tastes eternal peace. The joys
Springing from sense-life are but quickening wombs
Which breed sure griefs: those joys begin and end!
The wise mind takes no pleasure, Kunti's Son!
In such as those! But if a man shall learn,
Even while he lives and bears his body's chain,
To master lust and anger, he is blest!
He is the Yukta; he hath happiness,
Contentment, light, within: his life is merged
In Brahma's life; he doth Nirvana touch!
Thus go the Rishis unto rest, who dwell
With sins effaced, with doubts at end, with hearts
Governed and calm. Glad in all good they live,
Nigh to the peace of God; and all those live
Who pass their days exempt from greed and wrath,
Subduing self and senses, knowing the Soul!
The Saint who shuts outside his placid soul
All touch of sense, letting no contact through;
Whose quiet eyes gaze straight from fixed brows,
Whose outward breath and inward breath are drawn
Equal and slow through nostrils still and close;
That one-with organs, heart, and mind constrained,
Bent on deliverance, having put away
Passion, and fear, and rage;--hath, even now,
Obtained deliverance, ever and ever freed.
Yea! for he knows Me Who am He that heeds
The sacrifice and worship, God revealed;
And He who heeds not, being Lord of Worlds,
Lover of all that lives, God unrevealed,
Wherein who will shall find surety and shield!

HERE ENDS CHAPTER V. OF THE BHAGAVAD-GITA,
Entitled "Karmasanyasayog,"
Or "The Book of Religion by Renouncing Fruit of Works."
[1] That is,"joy and sorrow, success and failure, heat and cold,"&c.
[2] i.e., the body.

Six

Krishna.

> Therefore, who doeth work rightful to do,
> Not seeking gain from work, that man, O Prince!
> Is Sanyasi and Yogi--both in one
> And he is neither who lights not the flame
> Of sacrifice, nor setteth hand to task.
> Regard as true Renouncer him that makes
> Worship by work, for who renounceth not
> Works not as Yogin. So is that well said:
> "By works the votary doth rise to faith,
> And saintship is the ceasing from all works;
> Because the perfect Yogin acts--but acts
> Unmoved by passions and unbound by deeds,
> Setting result aside.
> Let each man raise
> The Self by Soul, not trample down his Self,
> Since Soul that is Self's friend may grow Self's foe.
> Soul is Self's friend when Self doth rule o'er Self,
> But Self turns enemy if Soul's own self
> Hates Self as not itself.[1]
> The sovereign soul
> Of him who lives self-governed and at peace
> Is centred in itself, taking alike
> Pleasure and pain; heat, cold; glory and shame.
> He is the Yogi, he is Yukta, glad
> With joy of light and truth; dwelling apart
> Upon a peak, with senses subjugate
> Whereto the clod, the rock, the glistering gold

Show all as one. By this sign is he known
Being of equal grace to comrades, friends,
Chance-comers, strangers, lovers, enemies,
Aliens and kinsmen; loving all alike,
Evil or good.
Sequestered should he sit,
Steadfastly meditating, solitary,
His thoughts controlled, his passions laid away,
Quit of belongings. In a fair, still spot
Having his fixed abode,--not too much raised,
Nor yet too low,--let him abide, his goods
A cloth, a deerskin, and the Kusa-grass.
There, setting hard his mind upon The One,
Restraining heart and senses, silent, calm,
Let him accomplish Yoga, and achieve
Pureness of soul, holding immovable
Body and neck and head, his gaze absorbed
Upon his nose-end,[2] rapt from all around,
Tranquil in spirit, free of fear, intent
Upon his Brahmacharya vow, devout,
Musing on Me, lost in the thought of Me.
That Yojin, so devoted, so controlled,
Comes to the peace beyond,--My peace, the peace
Of high Nirvana!
But for earthly needs
Religion is not his who too much fasts
Or too much feasts, nor his who sleeps away
An idle mind; nor his who wears to waste
His strength in vigils. Nay, Arjuna! call
That the true piety which most removes
Earth-aches and ills, where one is moderate
In eating and in resting, and in sport;
Measured in wish and act; sleeping betimes,
Waking betimes for duty.
When the man,
So living, centres on his soul the thought
Straitly restrained--untouched internally
By stress of sense--then is he Yukta. See!

Steadfast a lamp burns sheltered from the wind;
Such is the likeness of the Yogi's mind
Shut from sense-storms and burning bright to Heaven.
When mind broods placid, soothed with holy wont;
When Self contemplates self, and in itself
Hath comfort; when it knows the nameless joy
Beyond all scope of sense, revealed to soul--
Only to soul! and, knowing, wavers not,
True to the farther Truth; when, holding this,
It deems no other treasure comparable,
But, harboured there, cannot be stirred or shook
By any gravest grief, call that state "peace,"
That happy severance Yoga; call that man
The perfect Yogin!
Steadfastly the will
Must toil thereto, till efforts end in ease,
And thought has passed from thinking. Shaking off
All longings bred by dreams of fame and gain,
Shutting the doorways of the senses close
With watchful ward; so, step by step, it comes
To gift of peace assured and heart assuaged,
When the mind dwells self-wrapped, and the soul broods
Cumberless. But, as often as the heart
Breaks--wild and wavering--from control, so oft
Let him re-curb it, let him rein it back
To the soul's governance; for perfect bliss
Grows only in the bosom tranquillised,
The spirit passionless, purged from offence,
Vowed to the Infinite. He who thus vows
His soul to the Supreme Soul, quitting sin,
Passes unhindered to the endless bliss
Of unity with Brahma. He so vowed,
So blended, sees the Life-Soul resident
In all things living, and all living things
In that Life-Soul contained. And whoso thus
Discerneth Me in all, and all in Me,
I never let him go; nor looseneth he
Hold upon Me; but, dwell he where he may,

Whate'er his life, in Me he dwells and lives,
Because he knows and worships Me, Who dwell
In all which lives, and cleaves to Me in all.
Arjuna! if a man sees everywhere--
Taught by his own similitude--one Life,
One Essence in the Evil and the Good,
Hold him a Yogi, yea! well-perfected!
Arjuna.
Slayer of Madhu! yet again, this Yog,
This Peace, derived from equanimity,
Made known by thee--I see no fixity
Therein, no rest, because the heart of men
Is unfixed, Krishna! rash, tumultuous,
Wilful and strong. It were all one, I think,
To hold the wayward wind, as tame man's heart.
Krishna.
Hero long-armed! beyond denial, hard
Man's heart is to restrain, and wavering;
Yet may it grow restrained by habit, Prince!
By wont of self-command. This Yog, I say,
Cometh not lightly to th' ungoverned ones;
But he who will be master of himself
Shall win it, if he stoutly strive thereto.
Arjuna.
And what road goeth he who, having faith,
Fails, Krishna! in the striving; falling back
From holiness, missing the perfect rule?
Is he not lost, straying from Brahma's light,
Like the vain cloud, which floats 'twixt earth and heaven
When lightning splits it, and it vanisheth?
Fain would I hear thee answer me herein,
Since, Krishna! none save thou can clear the doubt.

Description: I:\Geetai-Mission-2022\Edwin Arnold\3.jpg

Krishna.
He is not lost, thou Son of Pritha! No!
Nor earth, nor heaven is forfeit, even for him,
Because no heart that holds one right desire
Treadeth the road of loss! He who should fail,
Desiring righteousness, cometh at death
Unto the Region of the Just; dwells there
Measureless years, and being born anew,
Beginneth life again in some fair home
Amid the mild and happy. It may chance
He doth descend into a Yogin house
On Virtue's breast; but that is rare! Such birth
Is hard to be obtained on this earth, Chief!
So hath he back again what heights of heart
He did achieve, and so he strives anew
To perfectness, with better hope, dear Prince!
For by the old desire he is drawn on
Unwittingly; and only to desire
The purity of Yog is to pass
Beyond the Sabdabrahm, the spoken Ved.
But, being Yogi, striving strong and long,

Purged from transgressions, perfected by births
Following on births, he plants his feet at last
Upon the farther path. Such as one ranks
Above ascetics, higher than the wise,
Beyond achievers of vast deeds! Be thou
Yogi Arjuna! And of such believe,
Truest and best is he who worships Me
With inmost soul, stayed on My Mystery!
HERE ENDETH CHAPTER VI. OF THE BHAGAVAD-GITA,
Entitled "Atmasanyamayog,"
Or "The Book of Religion by Self-Restraint."
[1] The Sanskrit has this play on the double meaning of Atman.
[2] *So in original.*

Seven

Krishna.

Learn now, dear Prince! how, if thy soul be set
Ever on Me--still exercising Yog,
Still making Me thy Refuge--thou shalt come
Most surely unto perfect hold of Me.
I will declare to thee that utmost lore,
Whole and particular, which, when thou knowest,
Leaveth no more to know here in this world.
Of many thousand mortals, one, perchance,
Striveth for Truth; and of those few that strive--
Nay, and rise high--one only--here and there--
Knoweth Me, as I am, the very Truth.
Earth, water, flame, air, ether, life, and mind,
And individuality--those eight
Make up the showing of Me, Manifest.
These be my lower Nature; learn the higher,
Whereby, thou Valiant One! this Universe
Is, by its principle of life, produced;
Whereby the worlds of visible things are born
As from a Yoni. Know! I am that womb:
I make and I unmake this Universe:
Than me there is no other Master, Prince!
No other Maker! All these hang on me
As hangs a row of pearls upon its string.
I am the fresh taste of the water; I
The silver of the moon, the gold o' the sun,
The word of worship in the Veds, the thrill
That passeth in the ether, and the strength

Of man's shed seed. I am the good sweet smell
Of the moistened earth, I am the fire's red light,
The vital air moving in all which moves,
The holiness of hallowed souls, the root
Undying, whence hath sprung whatever is;
The wisdom of the wise, the intellect
Of the informed, the greatness of the great.
The splendour of the splendid. Kunti's Son!
These am I, free from passion and desire;
Yet am I right desire in all who yearn,
Chief of the Bharatas! for all those moods,
Soothfast, or passionate, or ignorant,
Which Nature frames, deduce from me; but all
Are merged in me--not I in them! The world--
Deceived by those three qualities of being--
Wotteth not Me Who am outside them all,
Above them all, Eternal! Hard it is
To pierce that veil divine of various shows
Which hideth Me; yet they who worship Me
Pierce it and pass beyond.
I am not known
To evil-doers, nor to foolish ones,
Nor to the base and churlish; nor to those
Whose mind is cheated by the show of things,
Nor those that take the way of Asuras.[1]
Four sorts of mortals know me: he who weeps,
Arjuna! and the man who yearns to know;
And he who toils to help; and he who sits
Certain of me, enlightened.
Of these four,
O Prince of India! highest, nearest, best
That last is, the devout soul, wise, intent
Upon "The One." Dear, above all, am I
To him; and he is dearest unto me!
All four are good, and seek me; but mine own,
The true of heart, the faithful--stayed on me,
Taking me as their utmost blessedness,
They are not "mine,"but I--even I myself!

At end of many births to Me they come!
Yet hard the wise Mahatma is to find,
That man who sayeth, "All is Vasudev!"[2]
There be those, too, whose knowledge, turned aside
By this desire or that, gives them to serve
Some lower gods, with various rites, constrained
By that which mouldeth them. Unto all such--
Worship what shrine they will, what shapes, in faith--
'Tis I who give them faith! I am content!
The heart thus asking favour from its God,
Darkened but ardent, hath the end it craves,
The lesser blessing--but 'tis I who give!
Yet soon is withered what small fruit they reap:
Those men of little minds, who worship so,
Go where they worship, passing with their gods.
But Mine come unto me! Blind are the eyes
Which deem th' Unmanifested manifest,
Not comprehending Me in my true Self!
Imperishable, viewless, undeclared,
Hidden behind my magic veil of shows,
I am not seen by all; I am not known--
Unborn and changeless--to the idle world.
But I, Arjuna! know all things which were,
And all which are, and all which are to be,
Albeit not one among them knoweth Me!
By passion for the "pairs of opposites,"
By those twain snares of Like and Dislike, Prince!
All creatures live bewildered, save some few
Who, quit of sins, holy in act, informed,
Freed from the "opposites,"and fixed in faith,
Cleave unto Me.
Who cleave, who seek in Me
Refuge from birth[3] and death, those have the Truth!
Those know Me BRAHMA; know Me Soul of Souls,
The ADHYATMAN; know KARMA, my work;
Know I am ADHIBHUTA, Lord of Life,
And ADHIDAIVA, Lord of all the Gods,
And ADHIYAJNA, Lord of Sacrifice;

Worship Me well, with hearts of love and faith,
And find and hold me in the hour of death.
HERE ENDETH CHAPTER VII. OF THE BHAGAVAD-GITA,
Entitled "Vijnanayog,"
Or "The Book of Religion by Discernment."
[1] Beings of low and devilish nature.
[2] Krishna.
[3] I read here janma, "birth;" not jara,"age"

Eight

Arjuna.
Who is that BRAHMA? What that Soul of Souls,
The ADHYATMAN? What, Thou Best of All!
Thy work, the KARMA? Tell me what it is
Thou namest ADHIBHUTA? What again
Means ADHIDAIVA? Yea, and how it comes
Thou canst be ADHIYAJNA in thy flesh?
Slayer of Madhu! Further, make me know
How good men find thee in the hour of death?
Krishna.
I BRAHMA am! the One Eternal GOD,
And ADHYATMAN is My Being's name,
The Soul of Souls! What goeth forth from Me,
Causing all life to live, is KARMA called:
And, Manifested in divided forms,
I am the ADHIBHUTA, Lord of Lives;
And ADHIDAIVA, Lord of all the Gods,
Because I am PURUSHA, who begets.
And ADHIYAJNA, Lord of Sacrifice,
I--speaking with thee in this body here--
Am, thou embodied one! (for all the shrines
Flame unto Me!) And, at the hour of death,
He that hath meditated Me alone,
In putting off his flesh, comes forth to Me,
Enters into My Being--doubt thou not!
But, if he meditated otherwise
At hour of death, in putting off the flesh,
He goes to what he looked for, Kunti's Son!

Because the Soul is fashioned to its like.
Have Me, then, in thy heart always! and fight!
Thou too, when heart and mind are fixed on Me,
Shalt surely come to Me! All come who cleave
With never-wavering will of firmest faith,
Owning none other Gods: all come to Me,
The Uttermost, Purusha, Holiest!
Whoso hath known Me, Lord of sage and singer,
Ancient of days; of all the Three Worlds Stay,
Boundless,--but unto every atom Bringer
Of that which quickens it: whoso, I say,
Hath known My form, which passeth mortal knowing;
Seen my effulgence--which no eye hath seen--
Than the sun's burning gold more brightly glowing,
Dispersing darkness,--unto him hath been
Right life! And, in the hour when life is ending,
With mind set fast and trustful piety,
Drawing still breath beneath calm brows unbending,
In happy peace that faithful one doth die,--
In glad peace passeth to Purusha's heaven.
The place which they who read the Vedas name
AKSHARAM, "Ultimate;" whereto have striven
Saints and ascetics--their road is the same.
That way--the highest way--goes he who shuts
The gates of all his senses, locks desire
Safe in his heart, centres the vital airs
Upon his parting thought, steadfastly set;
And, murmuring OM, the sacred syllable--
Emblem of BRAHM--dies, meditating Me.
For who, none other Gods regarding, looks
Ever to Me, easily am I gained
By such a Yogi; and, attaining Me,
They fall not--those Mahatmas--back to birth,
To life, which is the place of pain, which ends,
But take the way of utmost blessedness.
The worlds, Arjuna!--even Brahma's world--
Roll back again from Death to Life's unrest;
But they, O Kunti's Son! that reach to Me,

Taste birth no more. If ye know Brahma's Day
Which is a thousand Yugas; if ye know
The thousand Yugas making Brahma's Night,
Then know ye Day and Night as He doth know!
When that vast Dawn doth break, th' Invisible
Is brought anew into the Visible;
When that deep Night doth darken, all which is
Fades back again to Him Who sent it forth;
Yea! this vast company of living things--
Again and yet again produced--expires
At Brahma's Nightfall; and, at Brahma's Dawn,
Riseth, without its will, to life new-born.
But--higher, deeper, innermost--abides
Another Life, not like the life of sense,
Escaping sight, unchanging. This endures
When all created things have passed away:
This is that Life named the Unmanifest,
The Infinite! the All! the Uttermost.
Thither arriving none return. That Life
Is Mine, and I am there! And, Prince! by faith
Which wanders not, there is a way to come
Thither. I, the PURUSHA, I Who spread
The Universe around me--in Whom dwell
All living Things--may so be reached and seen![1]
Richer than holy fruit on Vedas growing,
Greater than gifts, better than prayer or fast,
Such wisdom is! The Yogi, this way knowing,
Comes to the Utmost Perfect Peace at last.

Description: I:\Geetai-Mission-2022\Edwin Arnold\5.jpg

HERE ENDS CHAPTER IX. OF THE BHAGAVAD-GITA,
Entitled "Rajavidyarajaguhyayog,"
Or "The Book of Religion by the Kingly Knowledge and the Kingly
Mystery."
[1] I have discarded ten lines of Sanskrit text here as an undoubted
interpolation by some Vedantist

Nine

Krishna.

    Now will I open unto thee--whose heart
    Rejects not--that last lore, deepest-concealed,
    That farthest secret of My Heavens and Earths,
    Which but to know shall set thee free from ills,--
    A royal lore! a Kingly mystery!
    Yea! for the soul such light as purgeth it
    From every sin; a light of holiness
    With inmost splendour shining; plain to see;
    Easy to walk by, inexhaustible!
    They that receive not this, failing in faith
    To grasp the greater wisdom, reach not Me,
    Destroyer of thy focs! They sink anew
    Into the realm of Flesh, where all things change!
    By Me the whole vast Universe of things
    Is spread abroad;--by Me, the Unmanifest!
    In Me are all existences contained;
    Not I in them!
    Yet they are not contained,
    Those visible things! Receive and strive to embrace
    The mystery majestical! My Being--
    Creating all, sustaining all--still dwells
    Outside of all!
    See! as the shoreless airs
    Move in the measureless space, but are not space,
    [And space were space without the moving airs];
    So all things are in Me, but are not I.
    At closing of each Kalpa, Indian Prince!

All things which be back to My Being come:
At the beginning of each Kalpa, all
Issue new-born from Me.
By Energy
And help of Prakriti my outer Self,
Again, and yet again, I make go forth
The realms of visible things--without their will--
All of them--by the power of Prakriti.
Yet these great makings, Prince! involve Me not
Enchain Me not! I sit apart from them,
Other, and Higher, and Free; nowise attached!
Thus doth the stuff of worlds, moulded by Me,
Bring forth all that which is, moving or still,
Living or lifeless! Thus the worlds go on!
The minds untaught mistake Me, veiled in form;--
Naught see they of My secret Presence, nought
Of My hid Nature, ruling all which lives.
Vain hopes pursuing, vain deeds doing; fed
On vainest knowledge, senselessly they seek
An evil way, the way of brutes and fiends.
But My Mahatmas, those of noble soul
Who tread the path celestial, worship Me
With hearts unwandering,--knowing Me the Source,
Th' Eternal Source, of Life. Unendingly
They glorify Me; seek Me; keep their vows
Of reverence and love, with changeless faith
Adoring Me. Yea, and those too adore,
Who, offering sacrifice of wakened hearts,
Have sense of one pervading Spirit's stress,
One Force in every place, though manifold!
I am the Sacrifice! I am the Prayer!
I am the Funeral-Cake set for the dead!
I am the healing herb! I am the ghee,
The Mantra, and the flame, and that which burns!
I am-of all this boundless Universe-
The Father, Mother, Ancestor, and Guard!
The end of Learning! That which purifies
In lustral water! I am OM! I am

Rig-Veda, Sama-Veda, Yajur-Ved;
The Way, the Fosterer, the Lord, the Judge,
The Witness; the Abode, the Refuge-House,
The Friend, the Fountain and the Sea of Life
Which sends, and swallows up; Treasure of Worlds
And Treasure-Chamber! Seed and Seed-Sower,
Whence endless harvests spring! Sun's heat is mine;
Heaven's rain is mine to grant or to withhold;
Death am I, and Immortal Life I am,
Arjuna! SAT and ASAT, Visible Life,
And Life Invisible!
Yea! those who learn
The threefold Veds, who drink the Soma-wine,
Purge sins, pay sacrifice--from Me they earn
Passage to Swarga; where the meats divine
Of great gods feed them in high Indra's heaven.
Yet they, when that prodigious joy is o'er,
Paradise spent, and wage for merits given,
Come to the world of death and change once more.
They had their recompense! they stored their treasure,
Following the threefold Scripture and its writ;
Who seeketh such gaineth the fleeting pleasure
Of joy which comes and goes! I grant them it!
But to those blessed ones who worship Me,
Turning not otherwhere, with minds set fast,
I bring assurance of full bliss beyond.
Nay, and of hearts which follow other gods
In simple faith, their prayers arise to me,
O Kunti's Son! though they pray wrongfully;
For I am the Receiver and the Lord
Of every sacrifice, which these know not
Rightfully; so they fall to earth again!
Who follow gods go to their gods; who vow
Their souls to Pitris go to Pitris; minds
To evil Bhuts given o'er sink to the Bhuts;
And whoso loveth Me cometh to Me.
Whoso shall offer Me in faith and love
A leaf, a flower, a fruit, water poured forth,

That offering I accept, lovingly made
With pious will. Whate'er thou doest, Prince!
Eating or sacrificing, giving gifts,
Praying or fasting, let it all be done
For Me, as Mine. So shalt thou free thyself
From Karmabandh, the chain which holdeth men
To good and evil issue, so shalt come
Safe unto Me-when thou art quit of flesh--
By faith and abdication joined to Me!
I am alike for all! I know not hate,
I know not favour! What is made is Mine!
But them that worship Me with love, I love;
They are in Me, and I in them!
Nay, Prince!
If one of evil life turn in his thought
Straightly to Me, count him amidst the good;
He hath the high way chosen; he shall grow
Righteous ere long; he shall attain that peace
Which changes not. Thou Prince of India!
Be certain none can perish, trusting Me!
O Pritha's Son! whoso will turn to Me,
Though they be born from the very womb of Sin,
Woman or man; sprung of the Vaisya caste
Or lowly disregarded Sudra,--all
Plant foot upon the highest path; how then
The holy Brahmans and My Royal Saints?
Ah! ye who into this ill world are come--
Fleeting and false--set your faith fast on Me!
Fix heart and thought on Me! Adore Me! Bring
Offerings to Me! Make Me prostrations! Make
Me your supremest joy! and, undivided,
Unto My rest your spirits shall be guided.
HERE ENDS CHAPTER IX. OF THE BHAGAVAD-GITA,
Entitled "Rajavidyarajaguhyayog,"
Or "The Book of Religion by the Kingly Knowledge and the Kingly
Mystery."

Ten

Krishna.[1]

Hear farther yet, thou Long-Armed Lord! these latest words I say--
Uttered to bring thee bliss and peace, who lovest Me alway--
Not the great company of gods nor kingly Rishis know
My Nature, Who have made the gods and Rishis long ago;
He only knoweth-only he is free of sin, and wise,
Who seeth Me, Lord of the Worlds, with faith-enlightened eyes,
Unborn, undying, unbegun. Whatever Natures be
To mortal men distributed, those natures spring from Me!
Intellect, skill, enlightenment, endurance, self-control,
Truthfulness, equability, and grief or joy of soul,
And birth and death, and fearfulness, and fearlessness, and shame,
And honour, and sweet harmlessness,[2] and peace which is the same
Whate'er befalls, and mirth, and tears, and piety, and thrift,
And wish to give, and will to help,--all cometh of My gift!
The Seven Chief Saints, the Elders Four, the Lordly Manus set--
Sharing My work--to rule the worlds, these too did I beget;
And Rishis, Pitris, Manus, all, by one thought of My mind;
Thence did arise, to fill this world, the races of mankind;
Wherefrom who comprehends My Reign of mystic Majesty--
That truth of truths--is thenceforth linked in faultless faith to Me:
Yea! knowing Me the source of all, by Me all creatures wrought,
The wise in spirit cleave to Me, into My Being brought;
Hearts fixed on Me; breaths breathed to Me; praising Me, each to each,
So have they happiness and peace, with pious thought and speech;
And unto these--thus serving well, thus loving ceaselessly--
I give a mind of perfect mood, whereby they draw to Me;
And, all for love of them, within their darkened souls I dwell,

And, with bright rays of wisdom's lamp, their ignorance dispel.
Arjuna.
Yes! Thou art Parabrahm! The High Abode!
The Great Purification! Thou art God
Eternal, All-creating, Holy, First,
Without beginning! Lord of Lords and Gods!
Declared by all the Saints--by Narada,
Vyasa Asita, and Devalas;
And here Thyself declaring unto me!
What Thou hast said now know I to be truth,
O Kesava! that neither gods nor men
Nor demons comprehend Thy mystery
Made manifest, Divinest! Thou Thyself
Thyself alone dost know, Maker Supreme!
Master of all the living! Lord of Gods!
King of the Universe! To Thee alone
Belongs to tell the heavenly excellence
Of those perfections wherewith Thou dost fill
These worlds of Thine; Pervading, Immanent!
How shall I learn, Supremest Mystery!
To know Thee, though I muse continually?
Under what form of Thine unnumbered forms
Mayst Thou be grasped? Ah! yet again recount,
Clear and complete, Thy great appearances,
The secrets of Thy Majesty and Might,
Thou High Delight of Men! Never enough
Can mine ears drink the Amrit[3] of such words!
Krishna.
Hanta! So be it! Kuru Prince! I will to thee unfold
Some portions of My Majesty, whose powers are manifold!
I am the Spirit seated deep in every creature's heart;
From Me they come; by Me they live; at My word they depart!
Vishnu of the Adityas I am, those Lords of Light;
Maritchi of the Maruts, the Kings of Storm and Blight;
By day I gleam, the golden Sun of burning cloudless Noon;
By Night, amid the asterisms I glide, the dappled Moon!
Of Vedas I am Sama-Ved, of gods in Indra's Heaven
Vasava; of the faculties to living beings given

The mind which apprehends and thinks; of Rudras Sankara;
Of Yakshas and of Rakshasas, Vittesh; and Pavaka
Of Vasus, and of mountain-peaks Meru; Vrihaspati
Know Me 'mid planetary Powers; 'mid Warriors heavenly
Skanda; of all the water-floods the Sea which drinketh each,
And Bhrigu of the holy Saints, and OM of sacred speech;
Of prayers the prayer ye whisper;[4] of hills Himala's snow,
And Aswattha, the fig-tree, of all the trees that grow;
Of the Devarshis, Narada; and Chitrarath of them
That sing in Heaven, and Kapila of Munis, and the gem
Of flying steeds, Uchchaisravas, from Amrit-wave which burst;
Of elephants Airavata; of males the Best and First;
Of weapons Heav'n's hot thunderbolt; of cows white Kamadhuk,
From whose great milky udder-teats all hearts' desires are strook;
Vasuki of the serpent-tribes, round Mandara entwined;
And thousand-fanged Ananta, on whose broad coils reclined
Leans Vishnu; and of water-things Varuna; Aryam
Of Pitris, and, of those that judge, Yama the Judge I am;
Of Daityas dread Prahlada; of what metes days and years,
Time's self I am; of woodland-beasts-buffaloes, deers, and bears-
The lordly-painted tiger; of birds the vast Garud,
The whirlwind 'mid the winds; 'mid chiefs Rama with blood imbrued,
Makar 'mid fishes of the sea, and Ganges 'mid the streams;
Yea! First, and Last, and Centre of all which is or seems
I am, Arjuna! Wisdom Supreme of what is wise,
Words on the uttering lips I am, and eyesight of the eyes,
And "A" of written characters, Dwandwa[5] of knitted speech,
And Endless Life, and boundless Love, whose power sustaineth each;
And bitter Death which seizes all, and joyous sudden Birth,
Which brings to light all beings that are to be on earth;
And of the viewless virtues, Fame, Fortune, Song am I,
And Memory, and Patience; and Craft, and Constancy:
Of Vedic hymns the Vrihatsam, of metres Gayatri,
Of months the Margasirsha, of all the seasons three
The flower-wreathed Spring; in dicer's-play the conquering
Double-Eight;
The splendour of the splendid, and the greatness of the great,
Victory I am, and Action! and the goodness of the good,

And Vasudev of Vrishni's race, and of this Pandu brood
Thyself!--Yea, my Arjuna! thyself; for thou art Mine!
Of poets Usana, of saints Vyasa, sage divine;
The policy of conquerors, the potency of kings,
The great unbroken silence in learning's secret things;
The lore of all the learned, the seed of all which springs.
Living or lifeless, still or stirred, whatever beings be,
None of them is in all the worlds, but it exists by Me!
Nor tongue can tell, Arjuna! nor end of telling come
Of these My boundless glories, whereof I teach thee some;
For wheresoe'er is wondrous work, and majesty, and might,
From Me hath all proceeded. Receive thou this aright!
Yet how shouldst thou receive, O Prince! the vastness of this word?
I, who am all, and made it all, abide its separate Lord!
HERE ENDETH CHAPTER X. OF THE BHAGAVAD-GITA,
Entitled "Vibhuti Yog,"
Or "The Book of Religion by the Heavenly Perfections."

[1] The Sanskrit poem here rises to an elevation of style and manner which I have endeavoured to mark by change of metre.

[2] *Ahinsa.*

[3] The nectar of immortality.

[4] *Called "The Jap.".*

[5] *The compound form of Sanskrit words which often refer to a conflicting situation.*

Eleven

Arjuna.

This, for my soul's peace, have I heard from Thee,
The unfolding of the Mystery Supreme
Named Adhyatman; comprehending which,
My darkness is dispelled; for now I know--
O Lotus-eyed![1] --whence is the birth of men,
And whence their death, and what the majesties
Of Thine immortal rule. Fain would I see,
As thou Thyself declar'st it, Sovereign Lord!
The likeness of that glory of Thy Form
Wholly revealed. O Thou Divinest One!
If this can be, if I may bear the sight,
Make Thyself visible, Lord of all prayers!
Show me Thy very self, the Eternal God!
Krishna.
Gaze, then, thou Son of Pritha! I manifest for thee
Those hundred thousand thousand shapes that clothe my Mystery:
I show thee all my semblances, infinite, rich, divine,
My changeful hues, my countless forms. See! in this face of mine,
Adityas, Vasus, Rudras, Aswins, and Maruts; see
Wonders unnumbered, Indian Prince! revealed to none save thee.
Behold! this is the Universe!--Look! what is live and dead
I gather all in one--in Me! Gaze, as thy lips have said,
On GOD ETERNAL, VERY GOD! See Me! see what thou prayest!
Thou canst not!--nor, with human eyes, Arjuna! ever mayest!
Therefore I give thee sense divine. Have other eyes, new light!
And, look! This is My glory, unveiled to mortal sight!
Sanjaya.

Then, O King! the God, so saying,
Stood, to Pritha's Son displaying
All the splendour, wonder, dread
Of His vast Almighty-head.
Out of countless eyes beholding,
Out of countless mouths commanding,
Countless mystic forms enfolding
In one Form: supremely standing
Countless radiant glories wearing,
Countless heavenly weapons bearing,
Crowned with garlands of star-clusters,
Robed in garb of woven lustres,
Breathing from His perfect Presence
Breaths of every subtle essence
Of all heavenly odours; shedding
Blinding brilliance; overspreading--
Boundless, beautiful--all spaces
With His all-regarding faces;
So He showed! If there should rise
Suddenly within the skies
Sunburst of a thousand suns
Flooding earth with beams undeemed-of,
Then might be that Holy One's
Majesty and radiance dreamed of!
So did Pandu's Son behold
All this universe enfold
All its huge diversity
Into one vast shape, and be
Visible, and viewed, and blended
In one Body--subtle, splendid,
Nameless--th' All-comprehending
God of Gods, the Never-Ending
Deity!
But, sore amazed,
Thrilled, o'erfilled, dazzled, and dazed,
Arjuna knelt; and bowed his head,
And clasped his palms; and cried, and said:
Arjuna.

Yea! I have seen! I see!
Lord! all is wrapped in Thee!
The gods are in Thy glorious frame! the creatures
Of earth, and heaven, and hell
In Thy Divine form dwell,
And in Thy countenance shine all the features
Of Brahma, sitting lone
Upon His lotus-throne;
Of saints and sages, and the serpent races
Ananta, Vasuki;
Yea! mightiest Lord! I see
Thy thousand thousand arms, and breasts, and faces,
And eyes,--on every side
Perfect, diversified;
And nowhere end of Thee, nowhere beginning,
Nowhere a centre! Shifts--
Wherever soul's gaze lifts--
Thy central Self, all-wielding, and all-winning!
Infinite King! I see
The anadem on Thee,
The club, the shell, the discus; see Thee burning
In beams insufferable,
Lighting earth, heaven, and hell
With brilliance blazing, glowing, flashing; turning
Darkness to dazzling day,
Look I whichever way;
Ah, Lord! I worship Thee, the Undivided,
The Uttermost of thought,
The Treasure-Palace wrought
To hold the wealth of the worlds; the Shield provided
To shelter Virtue's laws;
The Fount whence Life's stream draws
All waters of all rivers of all being:
The One Unborn, Unending:
Unchanging and Unblending!
With might and majesty, past thought, past seeing!
Silver of moon and gold
Of sun are glories rolled

From Thy great eyes; Thy visage, beaming tender
Throughout the stars and skies,
Doth to warm life surprise
Thy Universe. The worlds are filled with wonder
Of Thy perfections! Space
Star-sprinkled, and void place
From pole to pole of the Blue, from bound to bound,
Hath Thee in every spot,
Thee, Thee!--Where Thou art not,
O Holy, Marvellous Form! is nowhere found!
O Mystic, Awful One!
At sight of Thee, made known,
The Three Worlds quake; the lower gods draw nigh Thee;
They fold their palms, and bow
Body, and breast, and brow,
And, whispering worship, laud and magnify Thee!
Rishis and Siddhas cry
"Hail! Highest Majesty!"
From sage and singer breaks the hymn of glory
In dulcet harmony,
Sounding the praise of Thee;
While countless companies take up the story,
Rudras, who ride the storms,
Th' Adityas' shining forms,
Vasus and Sadhyas, Viswas, Ushmapas;
Maruts, and those great Twins
The heavenly, fair, Aswins,
Gandharvas, Rakshasas, Siddhas, and Asuras,[2] --
These see Thee, and revere
In sudden-stricken fear;
Yea! the Worlds,--seeing Thee with form stupendous,
With faces manifold,
With eyes which all behold,
Unnumbered eyes, vast arms, members tremendous,
Flanks, lit with sun and star,
Feet planted near and far,
Tushes of terror, mouths wrathful and tender;--
The Three wide Worlds before Thee

Adore, as I adore Thee,
Quake, as I quake, to witness so much splendour!
I mark Thee strike the skies
With front, in wondrous wise
Huge, rainbow-painted, glittering; and thy mouth
Opened, and orbs which see
All things, whatever be
In all Thy worlds, east, west, and north and south.
O Eyes of God! O Head!
My strength of soul is fled,
Gone is heart's force, rebuked is mind's desire!
When I behold Thee so,
With awful brows a-glow,
With burning glance, and lips lighted by fire
Fierce as those flames which shall
Consume, at close of all,
Earth, Heaven! Ah me! I see no Earth and Heaven!
Thee, Lord of Lords! I see,
Thee only-only Thee!
Now let Thy mercy unto me be given,
Thou Refuge of the World!
Lo! to the cavern hurled
Of Thy wide-opened throat, and lips white-tushed,
I see our noblest ones,
Great Dhritarashtra's sons,
Bhishma, Drona, and Karna, caught and crushed!
The Kings and Chiefs drawn in,
That gaping gorge within;
The best of both these armies torn and riven!
Between Thy jaws they lie
Mangled full bloodily,
Ground into dust and death! Like streams down-driven
With helpless haste, which go
In headlong furious flow
Straight to the gulfing deeps of th' unfilled ocean,
So to that flaming cave
Those heroes great and brave
Pour, in unending streams, with helpless motion!

Like moths which in the night
Flutter towards a light,
Drawn to their fiery doom, flying and dying,
So to their death still throng,
Blind, dazzled, borne along
Ceaselessly, all those multitudes, wild flying!
Thou, that hast fashioned men,
Devourest them again,
One with another, great and small, alike!
The creatures whom Thou mak'st,
With flaming jaws Thou tak'st,
Lapping them up! Lord God! Thy terrors strike
From end to end of earth,
Filling life full, from birth
To death, with deadly, burning, lurid dread!
Ah, Vishnu! make me know
Why is Thy visage so?
Who art Thou, feasting thus upon Thy dead?
Who? awful Deity!
I bow myself to Thee,
Namostu Te, Devavara! Prasid![3]
O Mightiest Lord! rehearse
Why hast Thou face so fierce?
Whence doth this aspect horrible proceed?
Krishna.
Thou seest Me as Time who kills,
Time who brings all to doom,
The Slayer Time, Ancient of Days, come hither to consume;
Excepting thee, of all these hosts of hostile chiefs arrayed,
There stands not one shall leave alive the battlefield! Dismayed
No longer be! Arise! obtain renown! destroy thy foes!
Fight for the kingdom waiting thee when thou hast vanquished those.
By Me they fall--not thee! the stroke of death is dealt them now,
Even as they show thus gallantly; My instrument art thou!
Strike, strong-armed Prince, at Drona! at Bhishma strike! deal death
On Karna, Jyadratha; stay all their warlike breath!
'Tis I who bid them perish! Thou wilt but slay the slain;
Fight! they must fall, and thou must live, victor upon this plain!

Sanjaya.
Hearing mighty Keshav's word,
Tremblingly that helmed Lord
Clasped his lifted palms, and--praying
Grace of Krishna--stood there, saying,
With bowed brow and accents broken,
These words, timorously spoken:
Arjuna.
Worthily, Lord of Might!
The whole world hath delight
In Thy surpassing power, obeying Thee;
The Rakshasas, in dread
At sight of Thee, are sped
To all four quarters; and the company
Of Siddhas sound Thy name.
How should they not proclaim
Thy Majesties, Divinest, Mightiest?
Thou Brahm, than Brahma greater!
Thou Infinite Creator!
Thou God of gods, Life's Dwelling-place and Rest!
Thou, of all souls the Soul!
The Comprehending Whole!
Of being formed, and formless being the Framer;
O Utmost One! O Lord!
Older than eld, Who stored
The worlds with wealth of life! O Treasure-Claimer,
Who wottest all, and art
Wisdom Thyself! O Part
In all, and All; for all from Thee have risen
Numberless now I see
The aspects are of Thee!
Vayu[4] Thou art, and He who keeps the prison
Of Narak, Yama dark;
And Agni's shining spark;
Varuna's waves are Thy waves. Moon and starlight
Are Thine! Prajapati
Art Thou, and 'tis to Thee
They knelt in worshipping the old world's far light,

The first of mortal men.
Again, Thou God! again
A thousand thousand times be magnified!
Honour and worship be--
Glory and praise,--to Thee
Namo, Namaste, cried on every side;
Cried here, above, below,
Uttered when Thou dost go,
Uttered where Thou dost come! Namo! we call;
Namostu! God adored!
Namostu! Nameless Lord!
Hail to Thee! Praise to Thee! Thou One in all;
For Thou art All! Yea, Thou!
Ah! if in anger now
Thou shouldst remember I did think Thee Friend,
Speaking with easy speech,
As men use each to each;
Did call Thee "Krishna," "Prince," nor comprehend
Thy hidden majesty,
The might, the awe of Thee;
Did, in my heedlessness, or in my love,
On journey, or in jest,
Or when we lay at rest,
Sitting at council, straying in the grove,
Alone, or in the throng,
Do Thee, most Holy! wrong,
Be Thy grace granted for that witless sin!
For Thou art, now I know,
Father of all below,
Of all above, of all the worlds within
Guru of Gurus; more
To reverence and adore
Than all which is adorable and high!
How, in the wide worlds three
Should any equal be?
Should any other share Thy Majesty?
Therefore, with body bent
And reverent intent,

I praise, and serve, and seek Thee, asking grace.
As father to a son,
As friend to friend, as one
Who loveth to his lover, turn Thy face
In gentleness on me!
Good is it I did see
This unknown marvel of Thy Form! But fear
Mingles with joy! Retake,
Dear Lord! for pity's sake
Thine earthly shape, which earthly eyes may bear!
Be merciful, and show
The visage that I know;
Let me regard Thee, as of yore, arrayed
With disc and forehead-gem,
With mace and anadem,
Thou that sustainest all things! Undismayed
Let me once more behold
The form I loved of old,
Thou of the thousand arms and countless eyes!
This frightened heart is fain
To see restored again
My Charioteer, in Krishna's kind disguise.
Krishna.
Yea! thou hast seen, Arjuna! because I loved thee well,
The secret countenance of Me, revealed by mystic spell,
Shining, and wonderful, and vast, majestic, manifold,
Which none save thou in all the years had favour to behold;
For not by Vedas cometh this, nor sacrifice, nor alms,
Nor works well-done, nor penance long, nor prayers, nor chaunted
psalms,
That mortal eyes should bear to view the Immortal Soul unclad,
Prince of the Kurus! This was kept for thee alone! Be glad!
Let no more trouble shake thy heart, because thine eyes have seen
My terror with My glory. As I before have been
So will I be again for thee; with lightened heart behold!
Once more I am thy Krishna, the form thou knew'st of old!
Sanjaya.
These words to Arjuna spake

Vasudev, and straight did take
Back again the semblance dear
Of the well-loved charioteer;
Peace and joy it did restore
When the Prince beheld once more
Mighty BRAHMA's form and face
Clothed in Krishna's gentle grace.
Arjuna.
Now that I see come back, Janardana!
This friendly human frame, my mind can think
Calm thoughts once more; my heart beats still again!
Krishna.
Yea! it was wonderful and terrible
To view me as thou didst, dear Prince! The gods
Dread and desire continually to view!
Yet not by Vedas, nor from sacrifice,
Nor penance, nor gift-giving, nor with prayer
Shall any so behold, as thou hast seen!
Only by fullest service, perfect faith,
And uttermost surrender am I known
And seen, and entered into, Indian Prince!
Who doeth all for Me; who findeth Me
In all; adoreth always; loveth all
Which I have made, and Me, for Love's sole end
That man, Arjuna! unto Me doth wend.
HERE ENDETH CHAPTER XI. OF THE BHAGAVAD-GITA,
Entitled "Viswarupadarsanam,"
[1] "Kamalapatraksha".
[2] *These are all divine or deified orders of the Hindoo Pantheon.*
[3] "Hail to Thee, God of Gods! Be favourable!"
[4] The wind.

Twelve

Arjuna.

Lord! of the men who serve Thee--true in heart--
As God revealed; and of the men who serve,
Worshipping Thee Unrevealed, Unbodied, Far,
Which take the better way of faith and life?

Krishna.

Whoever serve Me--as I show Myself--
Constantly true, in full devotion fixed,
Those hold I very holy. But who serve--
Worshipping Me The One, The Invisible,
The Unrevealed, Unnamed, Unthinkable,
Uttermost, All-pervading, Highest, Sure--
Who thus adore Me, mastering their sense,
Of one set mind to all, glad in all good,
These blessed souls come unto Me.
Yet, hard
The travail is for such as bend their minds
To reach th' Unmanifest That viewless path
Shall scarce be trod by man bearing the flesh!
But whereso any doeth all his deeds
Renouncing self for Me, full of Me, fixed
To serve only the Highest, night and day
Musing on Me--him will I swiftly lift
Forth from life's ocean of distress and death,
Whose soul clings fast to Me. Cling thou to Me!
Clasp Me with heart and mind! so shalt thou dwell
Surely with Me on high. But if thy thought
Droops from such height; if thou be'st weak to set

Body and soul upon Me constantly,
Despair not! give Me lower service! seek
To reach Me, worshipping with steadfast will;
And, if thou canst not worship steadfastly,
Work for Me, toil in works pleasing to Me!
For he that laboureth right for love of Me
Shall finally attain! But, if in this
Thy faint heart fails, bring Me thy failure! find
Refuge in Me! let fruits of labour go,
Renouncing hope for Me, with lowliest heart,
So shalt thou come; for, though to know is more
Than diligence, yet worship better is
Than knowing, and renouncing better still.
Near to renunciation--very near--
Dwelleth Eternal Peace!
Who hateth nought
Of all which lives, living himself benign,
Compassionate, from arrogance exempt,
Exempt from love of self, unchangeable
By good or ill; patient, contented, firm
In faith, mastering himself, true to his word,
Seeking Me, heart and soul; vowed unto Me,--
That man I love! Who troubleth not his kind,
And is not troubled by them; clear of wrath,
Living too high for gladness, grief, or fear,
That man I love! Who, dwelling quiet-eyed,[1]
Stainless, serene, well-balanced, unperplexed,
Working with Me, yet from all works detached,
That man I love! Who, fixed in faith on Me,
Dotes upon none, scorns none; rejoices not,
And grieves not, letting good or evil hap
Light when it will, and when it will depart,
That man I love! Who, unto friend and foe
Keeping an equal heart, with equal mind
Bears shame and glory; with an equal peace
Takes heat and cold, pleasure and pain; abides
Quit of desires, hears praise or calumny
In passionless restraint, unmoved by each;

Linked by no ties to earth, steadfast in Me,
That man I love! But most of all I love
Those happy ones to whom 'tis life to live
In single fervid faith and love unseeing,
Drinking the blessed Amrit of my Being!
HERE ENDETH CHAPTER XII. OF THE BHAGAVAD-GITA,
Entitled "Bhaktiyog,"
Or"The Book of the Religion of Faith."
[1] "Not peering about,"anapeksha.

Thirteen

Arjuna.

Now would I hear, O gracious Kesava![1]
Of Life which seems, and Soul beyond, which sees,
And what it is we know-or think to know.
Krishna.
Yea! Son of Kunti! for this flesh ye see
Is Kshetra, is the field where Life disports;
And that which views and knows it is the Soul,
Kshetrajna. In all "fields," thou Indian prince!
I am Kshetrajna. I am what surveys!
Only that knowledge knows which knows the known
By the knower![2] What it is, that "field" of life,
What qualities it hath, and whence it is,
And why it changeth, and the faculty
That wotteth it, the mightiness of this,
And how it wotteth-hear these things from Me![3]
The elements, the conscious life, the mind,
The unseen vital force, the nine strange gates
Of the body, and the five domains of sense;
Desire, dislike, pleasure and pain, and thought
Deep-woven, and persistency of being;
These all are wrought on Matter by the Soul!
Humbleness, truthfulness, and harmlessness,
Patience and honour, reverence for the wise.
Purity, constancy, control of self,
Contempt of sense-delights, self-sacrifice,
Perception of the certitude of ill
In birth, death, age, disease, suffering, and sin;

Detachment, lightly holding unto home,
Children, and wife, and all that bindeth men;
An ever-tranquil heart in fortunes good
And fortunes evil, with a will set firm
To worship Me--Me only! ceasing not;
Loving all solitudes, and shunning noise
Of foolish crowds; endeavours resolute
To reach perception of the Utmost Soul,
And grace to understand what gain it were
So to attain,--this is true Wisdom, Prince!
And what is otherwise is ignorance!
Now will I speak of knowledge best to know-
That Truth which giveth man Amrit to drink,
The Truth of HIM, the Para-Brahm, the All,
The Uncreated;; not Asat, not Sat,
Not Form, nor the Unformed; yet both, and more;--
Whose hands are everywhere, and everywhere
Planted His feet, and everywhere His eyes
Beholding, and His ears in every place
Hearing, and all His faces everywhere
Enlightening and encompassing His worlds.
Glorified in the senses He hath given,
Yet beyond sense He is; sustaining all,
Yet dwells He unattached: of forms and modes
Master, yet neither form nor mode hath He;
He is within all beings--and without--
Motionless, yet still moving; not discerned
For subtlety of instant presence; close
To all, to each; yet measurelessly far!
Not manifold, and yet subsisting still
In all which lives; for ever to be known
As the Sustainer, yet, at the End of Times,
He maketh all to end--and re-creates.
The Light of Lights He is, in the heart of the Dark
Shining eternally. Wisdom He is
And Wisdom's way, and Guide of all the wise,
Planted in every heart.
So have I told

Of Life's stuff, and the moulding, and the lore
To comprehend. Whoso, adoring Me,
Perceiveth this, shall surely come to Me!
Know thou that Nature and the Spirit both
Have no beginning! Know that qualities
And changes of them are by Nature wrought;
That Nature puts to work the acting frame,
But Spirit doth inform it, and so cause
Feeling of pain and pleasure. Spirit, linked
To moulded matter, entereth into bond
With qualities by Nature framed, and, thus
Married to matter, breeds the birth again
In good or evil yonis.[4]
Yet is this
Yea! in its bodily prison!--Spirit pure,
Spirit supreme; surveying, governing,
Guarding, possessing; Lord and Master still
PURUSHA, Ultimate, One Soul with Me.
Whoso thus knows himself, and knows his soul
PURUSHA, working through the qualities
With Nature's modes, the light hath come for him!
Whatever flesh he bears, never again
Shall he take on its load. Some few there be
By meditation find the Soul in Self
Self-schooled; and some by long philosophy
And holy life reach thither; some by works:
Some, never so attaining, hear of light
From other lips, and seize, and cleave to it
Worshipping; yea! and those--to teaching true--
Overpass Death!
Wherever, Indian Prince!
Life is--of moving things, or things unmoved,
Plant or still seed--know, what is there hath grown
By bond of Matter and of Spirit: Know
He sees indeed who sees in all alike
The living, lordly Soul; the Soul Supreme,
Imperishable amid the Perishing:
For, whoso thus beholds, in every place,

In every form, the same, one, Living Life,
Doth no more wrongfulness unto himself,
But goes the highest road which brings to bliss.
Seeing, he sees, indeed, who sees that works
Are Nature's wont, for Soul to practise by
Acting, yet not the agent; sees the mass
Of separate living things--each of its kind--
Issue from One, and blend again to One:
Then hath he BRAHMA, he attains!
O Prince!
That Ultimate, High Spirit, Uncreate,
Unqualified, even when it entereth flesh
Taketh no stain of acts, worketh in nought!
Like to the ethereal air, pervading all,
Which, for sheer subtlety, avoideth taint,
The subtle Soul sits everywhere, unstained:
Like to the light of the all-piercing sun
[Which is not changed by aught it shines upon,]
The Soul's light shineth pure in every place;
And they who, by such eye of wisdom, see
How Matter, and what deals with it, divide;
And how the Spirit and the flesh have strife,
Those wise ones go the way which leads to Life!
HERE ENDS CHAPTER XIII. OF THE BHAGAVAD-GITA,
Entitled "Kshetrakshetrajnavibhagayog,"
Or "The Book of Religion by Separation of Matter and Spirit."

[1] The Calcutta edition of the Mahabharata has these three opening lines.

[2] This is the nearest possible version of Kshetrakshetrajnayojnanan yat tajnan matan mama.

[3] I omit two lines of the Sanskrit here, evidently interpolated by some Vedantist.

[4] Wombs.

Fourteen

Krishna.

    Yet farther will I open unto thee
This wisdom of all wisdoms, uttermost,
The which possessing, all My saints have passed
To perfectness. On such high verities
Reliant, rising into fellowship
With Me, they are not born again at birth
Of Kalpas, nor at Pralyas suffer change!
This Universe the womb is where I plant
Seed of all lives! Thence, Prince of India, comes
Birth to all beings! Whoso, Kunti's Son!
Mothers each mortal form, Brahma conceives,
And I am He that fathers, sending seed!
Sattwan, Rajas, and Tamas, so are named
The qualities of Nature, "Soothfastness,"
"Passion," and "Ignorance." These three bind down
The changeless Spirit in the changeful flesh.
Whereof sweet "Soothfastness," by purity
Living unsullied and enlightened, binds
The sinless Soul to happiness and truth;
And Passion, being kin to appetite,
And breeding impulse and propensity,
Binds the embodied Soul, O Kunti's Son!
By tie of works. But Ignorance, begot
Of Darkness, blinding mortal men, binds down
Their souls to stupor, sloth, and drowsiness.
Yea, Prince of India! Soothfastness binds souls
In pleasant wise to flesh; and Passion binds

By toilsome strain; but Ignorance, which blots
The beams of wisdom, binds the soul to sloth.
Passion and Ignorance, once overcome,
Leave Soothfastness, O Bharata! Where this
With Ignorance are absent, Passion rules;
And Ignorance in hearts not good nor quick.
When at all gateways of the Body shines
The Lamp of Knowledge, then may one see well
Soothfastness settled in that city reigns;
Where longing is, and ardour, and unrest,
Impulse to strive and gain, and avarice,
Those spring from Passion--Prince!--engrained; and where
Darkness and dulness, sloth and stupor are,
'Tis Ignorance hath caused them, Kuru Chief!
Moreover, when a soul departeth, fixed
In Soothfastness, it goeth to the place--
Perfect and pure--of those that know all Truth.
If it departeth in set habitude
Of Impulse, it shall pass into the world
Of spirits tied to works; and, if it dies
In hardened Ignorance, that blinded soul
Is born anew in some unlighted womb.
The fruit of Soothfastness is truc and sweet;
The fruit of lusts is pain and toil; the fruit
Of Ignorance is deeper darkness. Yea!
For Light brings light, and Passion ache to have;
And gloom, bewilderments, and ignorance
Grow forth from Ignorance. Those of the first
Rise ever higher; those of the second mode
Take a mid place; the darkened souls sink back
To lower deeps, loaded with witlessness!
When, watching life, the living man perceives
The only actors are the Qualities,
And knows what rules beyond the Qualities,
Then is he come nigh unto Me!
The Soul,
Thus passing forth from the Three Qualities--
Whereby arise all bodies--overcomes

Birth, Death, Sorrow, and Age; and drinketh deep
The undying wine of Amrit.
Arjuna.
Oh, my Lord!
Which be the signs to know him that hath gone
Past the Three Modes? How liveth he? What way
Leadeth him safe beyond the threefold Modes?
Krishna.
He who with equanimity surveys
Lustre of goodness, strife of passion, sloth
Of ignorance, not angry if they are,
Not wishful when they are not: he who sits
A sojourner and stranger in their midst
Unruffled, standing off, saying--serene--
When troubles break, "These be the Qualities!"
He unto whom--self-centred--grief and joy
Sound as one word; to whose deep-seeing eyes
The clod, the marble, and the gold are one;
Whose equal heart holds the same gentleness
For lovely and unlovely things, firm-set,
Well-pleased in praise and dispraise; satisfied
With honour or dishonour; unto friends
And unto foes alike in tolerance;
Detached from undertakings,--he is named
Surmounter of the Qualities!
And such--
With single, fervent faith adoring Me,
Passing beyond the Qualities, conforms
To Brahma, and attains Me!
For I am
That whereof Brahma is the likeness! Mine
The Amrit is; and Immortality
Is mine; and mine perfect Felicity!
HERE ENDS CHAPTER XIV. OF THE BHAGAVAD-GITA
Entitled "Gunatrayavibhagayog,"
Or "The Book of Religion by Separation from the Qualities."

Fifteen

Krishna.

 Men call the Aswattha,--the Banyan-tree,--
 Which hath its boughs beneath, its roots above,--
 The ever-holy tree. Yea! for its leaves
 Are green and waving hymns which whisper Truth!
 Who knows the Aswattha, knows Veds, and all.
 Its branches shoot to heaven and sink to earth,[1]
 Even as the deeds of men, which take their birth
 From qualities: its silver sprays and blooms,
 And all the eager verdure of its girth,
 Leap to quick life at kiss of sun and air,
 As men's lives quicken to the temptings fair
 Of wooing sense: its hanging rootlets seek
 The soil beneath, helping to hold it there,
 As actions wrought amid this world of men
 Bind them by ever-tightening bonds again.
 If ye knew well the teaching of the Tree,
 What its shape saith; and whence it springs; and, then
 How it must end, and all the ills of it,
 The axe of sharp Detachment ye would whet,
 And cleave the clinging snaky roots, and lay
 This Aswattha of sense-life low,--to set
 New growths upspringing to that happier sky,--
 Which they who reach shall have no day to die,
 Nor fade away, nor fall--to Him, I mean,
 FATHER and FIRST, Who made the mystery
 Of old Creation; for to Him come they
 From passion and from dreams who break away;

Who part the bonds constraining them to flesh,
And,--Him, the Highest, worshipping alway--
No longer grow at mercy of what breeze
Of summer pleasure stirs the sleeping trees,
What blast of tempest tears them, bough and stem
To the eternal world pass such as these!
Another Sun gleams there! another Moon!
Another Light,--not Dusk, nor Dawn, nor Noon--
Which they who once behold return no more;
They have attained My rest, life's Utmost boon!
When, in this world of manifested life,
The undying Spirit, setting forth from Me,
Taketh on form, it draweth to itself
From Being's storehouse,--which containeth all,--
Senses and intellect. The Sovereign Soul
Thus entering the flesh, or quitting it,
Gathers these up, as the wind gathers scents,
Blowing above the flower-beds. Ear and Eye,
And Touch and Taste, and Smelling, these it takes,--
Yea, and a sentient mind;--linking itself
To sense-things so.
The unenlightened ones
Mark not that Spirit when he goes or comes,
Nor when he takes his pleasure in the form,
Conjoined with qualities; but those see plain
Who have the eyes to see. Holy souls see
Which strive thereto. Enlightened, they perceive
That Spirit in themselves; but foolish ones,
Even though they strive, discern not, having hearts
Unkindled, ill-informed!
Know, too, from Me
Shineth the gathered glory of the suns
Which lighten all the world: from Me the moons
Draw silvery beams, and fire fierce loveliness.
I penetrate the clay, and lend all shapes
Their living force; I glide into the plant--
Root, leaf, and bloom--to make the woodlands green
With springing sap. Becoming vital warmth,

I glow in glad, respiring frames, and pass,
With outward and with inward breath, to feed
The body by all meats.[2]
For in this world
Being is twofold: the Divided, one;
The Undivided, one. All things that live
Are "the Divided." That which sits apart,
"The Undivided."
Higher still is He,
The Highest, holding all, whose Name is LORD,
The Eternal, Sovereign, First! Who fills all worlds,
Sustaining them. And--dwelling thus beyond
Divided Being and Undivided--I
Am called of men and Vedas, Life Supreme,
The PURUSHOTTAMA.
Who knows Me thus,
With mind unclouded, knoweth all, dear Prince!
And with his whole soul ever worshippeth Me.
Now is the sacred, secret Mystery
Declared to thee! Who comprehendeth this
Hath wisdom! He is quit of works in bliss!
HERE ENDS CHAPTER XV. OF THE BHAGAVAD-GITA
Entitled "Purushottamapraptiyog,"
Or "The Book of Religion by attaining the Supreme."

[1] I do not consider the Sanskrit verses here-which are somewhat freely rendered--"an attack on the authority of the Vedas," with Mr Davies, but a beautiful lyrical episode, a new "Parable of the fig-tree."

[2] I omit a verse here, evidently interpolated.

Sixteen

Krishna.

    Fearlessness, singleness of soul, the will
    Always to strive for wisdom; opened hand
    And governed appetites; and piety,
    And love of lonely study; humbleness,
    Uprightness, heed to injure nought which lives,
    Truthfulness, slowness unto wrath, a mind
    That lightly letteth go what others prize;
    And equanimity, and charity
    Which spieth no man's faults; and tenderness
    Towards all that suffer; a contented heart,
    Fluttered by no desires; a bearing mild,
    Modest, and grave, with manhood nobly mixed,
    With patience, fortitude, and purity;
    An unrevengeful spirit, never given
    To rate itself too high;--such be the signs,
    O Indian Prince! of him whose feet are set
    On that fair path which leads to heavenly birth!
    Deceitfulness, and arrogance, and pride,
    Quickness to anger, harsh and evil speech,
    And ignorance, to its own darkness blind,--
    These be the signs, My Prince! of him whose birth
    Is fated for the regions of the vile.[1]
    The Heavenly Birth brings to deliverance,
    So should'st thou know! The birth with Asuras
    Brings into bondage. Be thou joyous, Prince!
    Whose lot is set apart for heavenly Birth.
    Two stamps there are marked on all living men,

Divine and Undivine; I spake to thee
By what marks thou shouldst know the Heavenly Man,
Hear from me now of the Unheavenly!
They comprehend not, the Unheavenly,
How Souls go forth from Me; nor how they come
Back unto Me: nor is there Truth in these,
Nor purity, nor rule of Life. "This world
Hath not a Law, nor Order, nor a Lord,"
So say they: "nor hath risen up by Cause
Following on Cause, in perfect purposing,
But is none other than a House of Lust."
And, this thing thinking, all those ruined ones--
Of little wit, dark-minded--give themselves
To evil deeds, the curses of their kind.
Surrendered to desires insatiable,
Full of deceitfulness, folly, and pride,
In blindness cleaving to their errors, caught
Into the sinful course, they trust this lie
As it were true--this lie which leads to death--
Finding in Pleasure all the good which is,
And crying "Here it finisheth!"
Ensnared
In nooses of a hundred idle hopes,
Slaves to their passion and their wrath, they buy
Wealth with base deeds, to glut hot appetites;
"Thus much, to-day," they say, "we gained! thereby
Such and such wish of heart shall have its fill;
And this is ours! and th' other shall be ours!
To-day we slew a foe, and we will slay
Our other enemy to-morrow! Look!
Are we not lords? Make we not goodly cheer?
Is not our fortune famous, brave, and great?
Rich are we, proudly born! What other men
Live like to us? Kill, then, for sacrifice!
Cast largesse, and be merry!" So they speak
Darkened by ignorance; and so they fall--
Tossed to and fro with projects, tricked, and bound
In net of black delusion, lost in lusts--

Down to foul Naraka. Conceited, fond,
Stubborn and proud, dead-drunken with the wine
Of wealth, and reckless, all their offerings
Have but a show of reverence, being not made
In piety of ancient faith. Thus vowed
To self-hood, force, insolence, feasting, wrath,
These My blasphemers, in the forms they wear
And in the forms they breed, my foemen are,
Hateful and hating; cruel, evil, vile,
Lowest and least of men, whom I cast down
Again, and yet again, at end of lives,
Into some devilish womb, whence--birth by birth--
The devilish wombs re-spawn them, all beguiled;
And, till they find and worship Me, sweet Prince!
Tread they that Nether Road.
The Doors of Hell
Are threefold, whereby men to ruin pass,--
The door of Lust, the door of Wrath, the door
Of Avarice. Let a man shun those three!
He who shall turn aside from entering
All those three gates of Narak, wendeth straight
To find his peace, and comes to Swarga's gate.[2]
HERE ENDETH CHAPTER XVI. OF THE BHAGAVAD-GITA,
Entitled "Daivasarasaupadwibhagayog,"
Or "The Book of the Separateness of the Divine and Undivine."
[1] "Of the Asuras," lit.
[2] I omit the ten concluding shlokas, with Mr Davis.

Seventeen

Arjuna.

If men forsake the holy ordinance,
Heedless of Shastras, yet keep faith at heart
And worship, what shall be the state of those,
Great Krishna! Sattwan, Rajas, Tamas? Say!

Krishna.

Threefold the faith is of mankind and springs
From those three qualities,--becoming "true,"
Or "passion-stained," or "dark," as thou shalt hear!
The faith of each believer, Indian Prince!
Conforms itself to what he truly is.
Where thou shalt see a worshipper, that one
To what he worships lives assimilate,
[Such as the shrine, so is the votary,]
The "soothfast" souls adore true gods; the souls
Obeying Rajas worship Rakshasas[1]
Or Yakshas; and the men of Darkness pray
To Pretas and to Bhutas.[FN#35] Yea, and those
Who practise bitter penance, not enjoined
By rightful rule--penance which hath its root
In self-sufficient, proud hypocrisies--
Those men, passion-beset, violent, wild,
Torturing--the witless ones--My elements
Shut in fair company within their flesh,
(Nay, Me myself, present within the flesh!)
Know them to devils devoted, not to Heaven!
For like as foods are threefold for mankind
In nourishing, so is there threefold way

Of worship, abstinence, and almsgiving!
Hear this of Me! there is a food which brings
Force, substance, strength, and health, and joy to live,
Being well-seasoned, cordial, comforting,
The "Soothfast" meat. And there be foods which bring
Aches and unrests, and burning blood, and grief,
Being too biting, heating, salt, and sharp,
And therefore craved by too strong appetite.
And there is foul food--kept from over-night,[2]
Savourless, filthy, which the foul will eat,
A feast of rottenness, meet for the lips
Of such as love the "Darkness."
Thus with rites;--
A sacrifice not for rewardment made,
Offered in rightful wise, when he who vows
Sayeth, with heart devout, "This I should do!"
Is "Soothfast" rite. But sacrifice for gain,
Offered for good repute, be sure that this,
O Best of Bharatas! is Rajas-rite,
With stamp of "passion." And a sacrifice
Offered against the laws, with no due dole
Of food-giving, with no accompaniment
Of hallowed hymn, nor largesse to the priests,
In faithless celebration, call it vile,
The deed of "Darkness!"--lost!
Worship of gods
Meriting worship; lowly reverence
Of Twice-borns, Teachers, Elders; Purity,
Rectitude, and the Brahmacharya's vow,
And not to injure any helpless thing,--
These make a true religiousness of Act.
Words causing no man woe, words ever true,
Gentle and pleasing words, and those ye say
In murmured reading of a Sacred Writ,--
These make the true religiousness of Speech.
Serenity of soul, benignity,
Sway of the silent Spirit, constant stress
To sanctify the Nature,--these things make

Good rite, and true religiousness of Mind.
Such threefold faith, in highest piety
Kept, with no hope of gain, by hearts devote,
Is perfect work of Sattwan, true belief.
Religion shown in act of proud display
To win good entertainment, worship, fame,
Such--say I--is of Rajas, rash and vain.
Religion followed by a witless will
To torture self, or come at power to hurt
Another,--'tis of Tamas, dark and ill.
The gift lovingly given, when one shall say
"Now must I gladly give!" when he who takes
Can render nothing back; made in due place,
Due time, and to a meet recipient,
Is gift of Sattwan, fair and profitable.
The gift selfishly given, where to receive
Is hoped again, or when some end is sought,
Or where the gift is proffered with a grudge,
This is of Rajas, stained with impulse, ill.
The gift churlishly flung, at evil time,
In wrongful place, to base recipient,
Made in disdain or harsh unkindliness,
Is gift of Tamas, dark; it doth not bless![3]
HERE ENDETH CHAPTER XVII. OF THE BHAGAVAD-GITA,
Entitled "Sraddhatrayavibhagayog,"

[1] Rakshasas and Yakshas are unembodied but capricious beings of great power, gifts, and beauty, same times also of benignity.

[2] These are spirits of evil wandering ghosts.

[3] *I omit the concluding shlokas, as of very doubtful authenticity.*

Eighteen

Arjuna.

Fain would I better know, Thou Glorious One!
The very truth--Heart's Lord!--of Sannyas,
Abstention; and enunciation, Lord!
Tyaga; and what separates these twain!
Krishna.
The poets rightly teach that Sannyas
Is the foregoing of all acts which spring
Out of desire; and their wisest say
Tyaga is renouncing fruit of acts.
There be among the saints some who have held
All action sinful, and to be renounced;
And some who answer, "Nay! the goodly acts--
As worship, penance, alms--must be performed!"
Hear now My sentence, Best of Bharatas!
'Tis well set forth, O Chaser of thy Foes!
Renunciation is of threefold form,
And Worship, Penance, Alms, not to be stayed;
Nay, to be gladly done; for all those three
Are purifying waters for true souls!
Yet must be practised even those high works
In yielding up attachment, and all fruit
Produced by works. This is My judgment, Prince!
This My insuperable and fixed decree!
Abstaining from a work by right prescribed
Never is meet! So to abstain doth spring
From "Darkness," and Delusion teacheth it.
Abstaining from a work grievous to flesh,

When one saith "'Tis unpleasing!" this is null!
Such an one acts from "passion;" nought of gain
Wins his Renunciation! But, Arjun!
Abstaining from attachment to the work,
Abstaining from rewardment in the work,
While yet one doeth it full faithfully,
Saying, "Tis right to do!" that is "true " act
And abstinence! Who doeth duties so,
Unvexed if his work fail, if it succeed
Unflattered, in his own heart justified,
Quit of debates and doubts, his is "true" act:
For, being in the body, none may stand
Wholly aloof from act; yet, who abstains
From profit of his acts is abstinent.
The fruit of labours, in the lives to come,
Is threefold for all men,--Desirable,
And Undesirable, and mixed of both;
But no fruit is at all where no work was.
Hear from me, Long-armed Lord! the makings five
Which go to every act, in Sankhya taught
As necessary. First the force; and then
The agent; next, the various instruments;
Fourth, the especial effort; fifth, the God.
What work soever any mortal doth
Of body, mind, or speech, evil or good,
By these five doth he that. Which being thus,
Whoso, for lack of knowledge, seeth himself
As the sole actor, knoweth nought at all
And seeth nought. Therefore, I say, if one--
Holding aloof from self--with unstained mind
Should slay all yonder host, being bid to slay,
He doth not slay; he is not bound thereby!
Knowledge, the thing known, and the mind which knows,
These make the threefold starting-ground of act.
The act, the actor, and the instrument,
These make the threefold total of the deed.
But knowledge, agent, act, are differenced
By three dividing qualities. Hear now

Which be the qualities dividing them.
There is "true" Knowledge. Learn thou it is this:
To see one changeless Life in all the Lives,
And in the Separate, One Inseparable.
There is imperfect Knowledge: that which sees
The separate existences apart,
And, being separated, holds them real.
There is false Knowledge: that which blindly clings
To one as if 'twere all, seeking no Cause,
Deprived of light, narrow, and dull, and "dark."
There is "right" Action: that which being enjoined--
Is wrought without attachment, passionlessly,
For duty, not for love, nor hate, nor gain.
There is "vain" Action: that which men pursue
Aching to satisfy desires, impelled
By sense of self, with all-absorbing stress:
This is of Rajas--passionate and vain.
There is "dark" Action: when one doth a thing
Heedless of issues, heedless of the hurt
Or wrong for others, heedless if he harm
His own soul--'tis of Tamas, black and bad!
There is the "rightful"doer. He who acts
Free from self-seeking, humble, resolute,
Steadfast, in good or evil hap the same,
Content to do aright-he "truly" acts.
There is th' "impassioned" doer. He that works
From impulse, seeking profit, rude and bold
To overcome, unchastened; slave by turns
Of sorrow and of joy: of Rajas he!
And there be evil doers; loose of heart,
Low-minded, stubborn, fraudulent, remiss,
Dull, slow, despondent--children of the "dark."
Hear, too, of Intellect and Steadfastness
The threefold separation, Conqueror-Prince!
How these are set apart by Qualities.
Good is the Intellect which comprehends
The coming forth and going back of life,
What must be done, and what must not be done,

What should be feared, and what should not be feared,
What binds and what emancipates the soul:
That is of Sattwan, Prince! of "soothfastness."
Marred is the Intellect which, knowing right
And knowing wrong, and what is well to do
And what must not be done, yet understands
Nought with firm mind, nor as the calm truth is:
This is of Rajas, Prince! and "passionate!"
Evil is Intellect which, wrapped in gloom,
Looks upon wrong as right, and sees all things
Contrariwise of Truth. O Pritha's Son!
That is of Tamas, "dark" and desperate!
Good is the steadfastness whereby a man
Masters his beats of heart, his very breath
Of life, the action of his senses; fixed
In never-shaken faith and piety:
That is of Sattwan, Prince! "soothfast" and fair!
Stained is the steadfastness whereby a man
Holds to his duty, purpose, effort, end,
For life's sake, and the love of goods to gain,
Arjuna! 'tis of Rajas, passion-stamped!
Sad is the steadfastness wherewith the fool
Cleaves to his sloth, his sorrow, and his fears,
His folly and despair. This--Pritha's Son!--
Is born of Tamas, "dark" and miserable!
Hear further, Chief of Bharatas! from Me
The threefold kinds of Pleasure which there be.
Good Pleasure is the pleasure that endures,
Banishing pain for aye; bitter at first
As poison to the soul, but afterward
Sweet as the taste of Amrit. Drink of that!
It springeth in the Spirit's deep content.
And painful Pleasure springeth from the bond
Between the senses and the sense-world. Sweet
As Amrit is its first taste, but its last
Bitter as poison. 'Tis of Rajas, Prince!
And foul and "dark" the Pleasure is which springs
From sloth and sin and foolishness; at first

And at the last, and all the way of life
The soul bewildering. 'Tis of Tamas, Prince!
For nothing lives on earth, nor 'midst the gods
In utmost heaven, but hath its being bound
With these three Qualities, by Nature framed.
The work of Brahmans, Kshatriyas, Vaisyas,
And Sudras, O thou Slayer of thy Foes!
Is fixed by reason of the Qualities
Planted in each:
A Brahman's virtues, Prince!
Born of his nature, are serenity,
Self-mastery, religion, purity,
Patience, uprightness, learning, and to know
The truth of things which be. A Kshatriya's pride,
Born of his nature, lives in valour, fire,
Constancy, skilfulness, spirit in fight,
And open-handedness and noble mien,
As of a lord of men. A Vaisya's task,
Born with his nature, is to till the ground,
Tend cattle, venture trade. A Sudra's state,
Suiting his nature, is to minister.
Whoso performeth--diligent, content--
The work allotted him, whate'er it be,
Lays hold of perfectness! Hear how a man
Findeth perfection, being so content:
He findeth it through worship--wrought by work--
Of Him that is the Source of all which lives,
Of HIM by Whom the universe was stretched.
Better thine own work is, though done with fault,
Than doing others' work, ev'n excellently.
He shall not fall in sin who fronts the task
Set him by Nature's hand! Let no man leave
His natural duty, Prince! though it bear blame!
For every work hath blame, as every flame
Is wrapped in smoke! Only that man attains
Perfect surcease of work whose work was wrought
With mind unfettered, soul wholly subdued,
Desires for ever dead, results renounced.

Learn from me, Son of Kunti! also this,
How one, attaining perfect peace, attains
BRAHM, the supreme, the highest height of all!
Devoted--with a heart grown pure, restrained
In lordly self-control, forgoing wiles
Of song and senses, freed from love and hate,
Dwelling 'mid solitudes, in diet spare,
With body, speech, and will tamed to obey,
Ever to holy meditation vowed,
From passions liberate, quit of the Self,
Of arrogance, impatience, anger, pride;
Freed from surroundings, quiet, lacking nought--
Such an one grows to oneness with the BRAHM;
Such an one, growing one with BRAHM, serene,
Sorrows no more, desires no more; his soul,
Equally loving all that lives, loves well
Me, Who have made them, and attains to Me.
By this same love and worship doth he know
Me as I am, how high and wonderful,
And knowing, straightway enters into Me.
And whatsoever deeds he doeth--fixed
In Me, as in his refuge--he hath won
For ever and for ever by My grace
Th' Eternal Rest! So win thou! In thy thoughts
Do all thou dost for Me! Renounce for Me!
Sacrifice heart and mind and will to Me!
Live in the faith of Me! In faith of Me
All dangers thou shalt vanquish, by My grace;
But, trusting to thyself and heeding not,
Thou can'st but perish! If this day thou say'st,
Relying on thyself, "I will not fight!"
Vain will the purpose prove! thy qualities
Would spur thee to the war. What thou dost shun,
Misled by fair illusions, thou wouldst seek
Against thy will, when the task comes to thee
Waking the promptings in thy nature set.
There lives a Master in the hearts of men
Maketh their deeds, by subtle pulling--strings,

Dance to what tune HE will. With all thy soul
Trust Him, and take Him for thy succour, Prince!
So--only so, Arjuna!--shalt thou gain--
By grace of Him--the uttermost repose,
The Eternal Place!
Thus hath been opened thee
This Truth of Truths, the Mystery more hid
Than any secret mystery. Meditate!
And--as thou wilt--then act!
Nay! but once more
Take My last word, My utmost meaning have!
Precious thou art to Me; right well-beloved!
Listen! I tell thee for thy comfort this.
Give Me thy heart! adore Me! serve Me! cling
In faith and love and reverence to Me!
So shalt thou come to Me! I promise true,
For thou art sweet to Me!
And let go those--
Rites and writ duties! Fly to Me alone!
Make Me thy single refuge! I will free
Thy soul from all its sins! Be of good cheer!
[Hide, the holy Krishna saith,
This from him that hath no faith,
Him that worships not, nor seeks
Wisdom's teaching when she speaks:
Hide it from all men who mock;
But, wherever, 'mid the flock
Of My lovers, one shall teach
This divinest, wisest, speech--
Teaching in the faith to bring
Truth to them, and offering
Of all honour unto Me--
Unto Brahma cometh he!
Nay, and nowhere shall ye find
Any man of all mankind
Doing dearer deed for Me;
Nor shall any dearer be
In My earth. Yea, furthermore,

Whoso reads this converse o'er,
Held by Us upon the plain,
Pondering piously and fain,
He hath paid Me sacrifice!
(Krishna speaketh in this wise!)
Yea, and whoso, full of faith,
Heareth wisely what it saith,
Heareth meekly,--when he dies,
Surely shall his spirit rise
To those regions where the Blest,
Free of flesh, in joyance rest.]
Hath this been heard by thee, O Indian Prince!
With mind intent? hath all the ignorance--
Which bred thy trouble--vanished, My Arjun?
Arjuna.
Trouble and ignorance are gone! the Light
Hath come unto me, by Thy favour, Lord!
Now am I fixed! my doubt is fled away!
According to Thy word, so will I do!
Sanjaya.
Thus gathered I the gracious speech of Krishna, O my King!
Thus have I told, with heart a-thrill, this wise and wondrous thing
By great Vyasa's learning writ, how Krishna's self made known
The Yoga, being Yoga's Lord. So is the high truth shown!
And aye, when I remember, O Lord my King, again
Arjuna and the God in talk, and all this holy strain,
Great is my gladness: when I muse that splendour, passing speech,
Of Hari, visible and plain, there is no tongue to reach
My marvel and my love and bliss. O Archer-Prince! all hail!
O Krishna, Lord of Yoga! surely there shall not fail
Blessing, and victory, and power, for Thy most mighty sake,
Where this song comes of Arjun, and how with God he spake.
HERE ENDS, WITH CHAPTER XVIII.,
Entitled "Mokshasanyasayog,"
Or "The Book of Religion by Deliverance and Renunciation,"
THE BHAGAVAD-GITA.

CHAPTER NINETEEN

Integrations of Yoga

As evident from the Gita, warrior Arjun lost his balance of mind after seeing his master, his elders and other relatives standing on the opponent's side. He refused to kill his masters and relatives simply for gaining a state. He even expressed his desire to cast off all his wishes to stop such a mass killing.

Saints intended to converge these philosophical ideals through conversation of the divine and individual duly displayed in the Gita. Integration of individual with Yoga is the core of the principle materialised in Gita with an aspiration of enabling a doer of actions in attainment of completeness by all means. The presentation of such conversation has also exhibited the existence of such Yoga philosophy from olden times in the universe. It has evolved differently in due course of time and also narrated differently by saints time to time. Gita was, obviously without any doubt, a successful efforts amongst all of them. Gita comprehends the teachings incorporated in Upanishads and Uanishads comprehend teachings prescribed in holy scritures like Vedas. It also links up the thought process of Vedantic, Yoga and Sankhya Philosophy of Indian origin. All these schools of thought process instruct an individual to lead a life on the basis of a divine goal of feeling the presence of sureme power by the side of immediate creations. All forms in this universe are nothing but the manifestation of the Divine. It is the only truth that can link up all the human beings throughout the world and can materialise the dream of a peaceful world order.

The comparative process of examining and assessing perfectness parameter is standing on the basis of certain directives usually made by a group of people. Because of that reason any perfectness parameter cannot claim that individuals moving through the screening of the perfectness examinations are absolutely perfect. We can work put billions of questions from any specific field of study. Moving through such a massive task might make the life of any aspirant a hell. The type of testing in the form of written interaction is usually made limited by incorporating a set of planned interactions and content areas with a pre – planned format of study.

CHAPTER TWENTY

Karma Yoga

Karma Yoga is often defined by thinkers and philosophers as "Yoga of Actions and Performance.[1]" "selfless actions perfomed by any individual for the benefit of others", on the other hand, as per narretives and postulated described in the Bhagavadgita, is considered as Karma Yoga.[2] Duties performed without maintaining aspiration of implying any claim on the result of fruit of action being performed leads an individual, with utmost contentment, to spiritual liberation.[3] Any work can be done with the spirit of a Karma Yogi as Karma Yoga.[4] Actions inflicted with, or more prominently to say in the context of the Bhagavadgita, driven by "equanimity, balance", with "dispassion, disinterest", avoiding "one sidedness, fear, craving, favoring self or one group or clan, self-pity, self-aggrandizement or any form of extreme reactiveness are the actions performed by a Karma yogi. Karma Yogi performs all the actions as the duty duly assigned by the nature to an individual and cannot maintain any claim on the results whatever comes out of the actions duly performed.[5] Selfless services performed with right feelings and positive attitude to serve the community, and ultimately to the nature to which the indibual belongs, is considered as Karma Yoga.[6] The action, which are categorised as Karma Yoga in the Holy Scripture the Gita, can be motivated by body or manipulated by external influences.[7] Even, with certain alteration, it can be motivated by one's inner reflection and true self (soul, Atman, Brahman).[8]

A person engaged in delivering services to others and performing duties duly assigned by the nature efficiently and properly moves towards an inward journey, in the other word spiritual enrichment (withdraw of senses from desires and compulsions and aspiring for spiritual contentment), which is inherently fulfilling and satisfying.[9] Seeker of rewarde for the duties performed may get inflicted with some sort of disappointment, frustrations or self-destructive apprehensions after completion of the work or in the middle.[10] Working without maintaining attachment to the actions, or without adhering to the fruit of actions one can easily move towards the supreme master and can feel the Divine omnipresence.[11]

Out of three means of liberation, Karma Yoga, as described in Sri Bhagavad Purana, is an easy way out. It can be followed by individuals while remaining at services and performing duties.[12] The first six chapters of the Bhagavadgita describe the essence of Karma Yoga in our daily life.[13]

Is there any liberty from Karma (performing duties or offering services to the nature or community) to a person who is aspiring to move towards complete renunciation? Absolutely, and speaking frankly without maintaining any alignment, No. one cannot escape different biological activities for remaining alive; the person is offering services to the nature, may be knowingly or unknowingly, while performing breathing, taking food and maintaining belongings. Karma Yoga is the part of life and can be judged as an inseparable part of life of all standatds and all levels. Offering services to other and also services to oneself is a part of daily activity which, at any cost and at any instance, cannot be avoided.

[1] P. T. Raju (1954), The Concept of the Spiritual in Indian Thought, Philosophy East and West, Vol. 4, No. 3 (Oct., 1954), pp. 210.

[2] James G. Lochtefeld (2002). The Illustrated Encyclopedia of Hinduism: A-M. The Rosen Publishing Group. p. 352. ISBN 978-0-8239-3179-8.

[3] Mulla, Zubin R.; Krishnan, Venkat R. (2013). "Karma-Yoga: The Indian Model of Moral Development". Journal of Business Ethics. Springer Nature. 123 (2): 342–345, context: 339–351. doi:10.1007/s10551-013-1842-8. S2CID 29065490.

[4] William L. Blizek (2009). The Continuum Companion to Religion and Film. Bloomsbury Academic. pp. 161–162. ISBN 978-0-8264-9991-2.

[5] Harold G. Coward (2012). Perfectibility of Human Nature in Eastern and Western Thought, The. State University of New York Press. pp. 132–133. ISBN 978-0-7914-7885-1.

[6] Stephen Phillips (2009). Yoga, Karma, and Rebirth: A Brief History and Philosophy. Columbia University Press. pp. 99–100. ISBN 978-0-231-14485-8.

[7] The Bhagavadgita III.6 and III.8;

[8] Eliot Deutsch; Rohit Dalvi (2004). The Essential Vedanta: A New Source Book of Advaita Vedanta. World Wisdom. pp. 64–68. ISBN 978-0-941532-52-5.

[9] *Dharm Bhawuk (2011). Spirituality and Indian Psychology: Lessons from the Bhagavad-Gita. Springer Science. pp. 147–148 with footnotes. ISBN 978-1-4419-8110-3.*

[10] *Jonardon Ganeri (2007). The Concealed Art of the Soul: Theories of Self and Practices of Truth in Indian Ethics and Epistemology. Oxford University Press. pp. 67–69. ISBN 978-0-19-920241-6.*

[11] *"Bhagavad Gita 3.19". vedabase.io. Retrieved 3 November 2020.*

[12] *T.R. Sharma (2013). Karel Werner (ed.). Love Divine: Studies in 'Bhakti and Devotional Mysticism. Taylor & Francis. p. 85. ISBN 978-1-136-77468-3.*

[13] *Brian Hodgkinson (2006). The Essence of Vedanta. London: Arcturus. pp. 91–93. ISBN 978-1-84858-409-9.*

CHAPTER TWENTY-ONE

Bhakti Yoga

Bhakti Yoga is a spiritual path, more prominently to say, a way of life with focussed on loving devotion towards any personal deity.[1] It has ancient Uanishadic root, and also is considered as one of the three paths leading a person towards attainment of liberation from the cycle of birth and death.[2] The personal God varies with devotee considerably.[3] It is devotee's loving devotion to the personal God with an aspiration of growth in terms of spirituality.[4]

There are four types of devotees who practice Bhakti Yoga[5].

1. Devotees who are are pressed or stressed by anxiety or their daily life circumstances.
2. Devotee often aspires to learn about god out of curiosity and intellectual intrigue.
3. Some devotee seeks reward in this Yoga or in afterlife.
4. Some devotees continue expressing devotion to the master simply for devotion and for nothing else.

The traditional doctrines, as often termed as Shaivism in Indian tradition, teaches ethical living, service to the community and through one's work, loving worship, yoga practice and discipline, continuous learning and self-knowledge as means for liberating the individual soul from bondage.[6] This tradition also focussed condiderably on abstract ideas of spirituality.[7]

Instructuins on nine different types of devotion[8], as described in Bhagavad Purana and Ramayan, desplays the way a devotee can practice Bhakti Yoga: (1) śravaṇa ("listening" to the scriptural stories of Divine powers and their companions), (2) kīrtana ("praising"; generally and broadly refers to ecstatic group singing), (3) smaraṇa ("remembering" or fixing the mind on the Divine master; such master will from the collection of characters upon which the devotee is maintaining absolute faith), (4) pāda-sevana (rendering service to the lord or the creations made by the lord), (5) arcana (worshiping an idol, image or any other symbol which can represent the divine power in terms of physical status), (6) vandana (paying homage to the master), (7) dāsya (servitude without expecting anything in return), (8) sākhya (friendship with the divine master), and (9) ātma-nivedana (complete surrender of the self with an aspiration of seeking liberation from the world).

The perfect explanation of characters of a true devotee is propely presented in the context where Sage Veda Vyasa pointed out such features in chapter 12 of the Bhagavadgita. It was delivered by the divine master in the form of a synthesis of all the nine types of devotions as pointed out earlier in old scriptures.

Bhagavadgita (XII – 2 to 20)[9]

Quality of a devotee as preferred by the Divine master is described in this section.

1. Those who fix their minds on master and always engage in such state of devotion with steadfast faith will be considered as one of the best worshipper.

2. Those who worship the formless aspect of the Absolute Truth (the imperishable ones, the indefinable source, the all-pervading form, the unthinkable one, the unchanging type of the source of inspiration, the eternal, and the immoveable one) by restraining their senses, holding commands upon all the senses and by remaining even-minded everywhere, such progressive and balanced persons, while remaining engaged in the welfare of all beings, also without any doubt attain the Divine omnipresence.

3. Worship of the divine master will become easy for individuals having absolute focus on the goal of life.

4. Person worshipping the master without execting anything in return will pass through a state of liberation during which the divine master will deliver that devotee from the ocean of birth and death, for their consciousness is united with and is gradually becoming non-separable by any means.

5. Person gains the omnipresence of the divine master instantly if that devotee prepares to keep faith on the master alone and surrender the

very intellect to master. By doing so, devotee start always living in the beloved master.

6. Person having difficulties in remembering the divine master can have an alternative of fixing the mind steadily on master or alternatively on any other subject related to the divine master. Such devotee can practice remembering the fellow master with devotion while constantly restraining the mind from worldly affairs and also from other attachments.

7. Devotees having difficulties in remembering the divine master with devotion can simply try to work for the fellow master with utmost sinceerity. Thus performing devotional service to the master or to the subjects related to the master with continuation and prolonged regularity shall achieve the stage of perfection without any failure.

8. Another type of devotee can try to renounce the fruits of actions or duties duly performed in society and can attain utter contentment by focusing on the waves of the inner self.

9. A devotee knows well about the states of renunciation which is the best alternative of devotion. Knowledge is Better than mechanical practice; better than knowledge is meditation. Better than meditation is renunciation of the fruits of actions or results of duties delivered in society or to nature, for peace immediately follows attainment of such renunciation without any failure.

10. Those devotees are very dear to master who are free from malice toward all living beings, who are friendly in nature, and are also compassionate. They are free from attachment to possessions and egotism, equipoised in happiness and distress, and ever-forgiving one. They are ever-contented, steadily aligned to the side of the divine master and remain in absolute state of devotion; remain self-controlled, of firm resolve, and dedicated to the master in terms of mind, spirit and intellect.

1. The person capable enough in maintaining the sensible balance of body, mind and intellect with an aspiration of retaining the balanced state even during adversities; and who are equal in pleasure and pain, free from fear and anxiety; such devotees are the preferred one by the master.

2. Person keeping balance of mind and action during profit or loss, happiness or sorrow, good or evil deeds; and even retain balance of the mind during adversities are the real devotees.

Devotion impregnated with knowledge is considered as a best way out which leads an individual towards renunciation. Even absolute devotion without much knowledge can bring the same result of renunciation. Remaining loyal to the fellow master and considering all the instructions delivered by the master as final is the ultimate expectation that the Divine expects from an individual. This doctrine was explained in detail time to time in scriptures and epics through different events. Event related to mother SABARI, as was narrated by Sage Valmiki in RAMAYANA, is one of such example. True devotion never puts any argument and even never intends to indulge in any kind of dispute. It always rests upon the verdict of the Divine master and prepares to offer services to the nature at the will of the Divine. Such kind of living and dwelling brings absolute happiness for the devotee and inspires others for doing the same. There is a kind of absolute surrender with which a true devotee prepares oneself to reach the fellow master with an instantaneous pace. It also harnesses oneness of devotee and the Divine. Such a state is , and finally will be , the final destiny of an individual.

[1] Cutler, Norman (1987). Songs of Experience. Indiana University Press. pp. 1–2. ISBN 978-0-253-35334-4.

[2] Max Muller, Shvetashvatara Upanishad, The Upanishads, Part II, Oxford University Press, page 267

[3] Karen Pechelis (2011), Bhakti Traditions, in The Continuum Companion to Hindu Studies (Editors: Jessica Frazier, Gavin Flood), Bloomsbury, ISBN 978-0826499660, pages 107-121

[4] Gordon S. Wakefield (1983). The Westminster Dictionary of Christian Spirituality. WJK Press. pp. 46–47. ISBN 978-0-664-22170-6.

[5] Gordon S. Wakefield (1983). The Westminster Dictionary of Christian Spirituality. WJK Press. pp. 46–47. ISBN 978-0-664-22170-6.

[6] S Parmeshwaranand (2004). Encyclopaedia of the Śaivism. Sarup & Sons. pp. 210–217. ISBN 978-81-7625-427-4.

[7] Sanderson, Alexis (1988). "Saivism and the Tantric Traditions". In S Sutherland; et al. (eds.). The World's Religions. Routledge.

[8] Haberman, David L. (2001). Acting as a Way of Salvation. Motilal Banarsidass. pp. 133–134. ISBN 978-81-208-1794-4.

[9] Shri Madbhagavadgita Chater 12.

CHAPTER TWENTY-TWO

Jnana Yoga

Jnana Yoga emphasizes "the path of yoga meant primarily for assimilation and becoming enriched with knowledge."[1] This yoga primarily addresses the questions of an individual to actualise oneself in the realm of creations. Questions like: "Who am I", "What am I", "What is the goal of my life", etc. are some of such questions with which a person advances in this path.[2] The purpose of true knowledge is to attain liberation for the person aspiring for it.[3] The entire mechanism related to this path of yoga context is better understood, alon with some sort of examples and needful narratives, as "realization or gnosis", referring to a "path of study meant primarily for the attainment of liberation" wherein one knows the unity between self and ultimate reality called Brahman.[4] This path of knowledge is preferred by those who aspires for attaining some sort of advancement while delivering mental and spiritual services to the nature and also, with some brader apprehension, to the community.[5]

Enrichment of an individual in terms of attainment and utilisation of knowledge is an evercontinuing act. It will continue throughout the life of an individual. One can even assimilate knowledge with a normal day to day confluence by seeing the services and qualities of other natural objects. Entire nature, more perfectly to say in a brader sense, is filled with knowledge. One may attain such kinds of true knowledge without putting much effort. Realisation of oneness of an individual (ATMAN) with the Divine master (BRAHMAN) is the ultimate goal of JNANA YOGA.[6] The Bhagavadgita efficiently integrates the thought process of Sankhya, Vedanta and Yoga to explain the real goal of Jnana Yoga in the life of an individual. After knowling about the scince of such integration of individual and the Divine master one can feel the omnipresence of that supreme power. That supreme power is considered as a whole and the individual being aspires for gaining that totality and reverence through the path of Jnana Yoga.

Levels of emphasis may differ, but a worshipper of knowledge can have, and in actual sense must have, the combination of Karma Yoga and Devotion, to encompass the path leading towards liberation. One cannot claim at any instance that the person is exclusively or solely relying on Yoga of Knowledge (JNANA YOGA). It is even absurd to think and absolutely difficult to implement as the law of creation and biological processes cannot allow us to continue in the realm of creation without delivering some of the obligations. The related doctrine of Yoga of Knowledge is properly systematised earlier than Karma Yoga and Bhakti Yoga.[7] This yoga also offers an enlightenment to the soul with which the person start recognising the very self as an inseparable part of the nature, and finally as an inseparable part of the entire realm of the universal creation. The same individual is also a subject of the evergoing cycle of the creation and destruction, which will at any circumstances remain unavoidable.

The Bhagavadgita also emphasises that Divine master is the jīva śhakti (the soul energy), which comprises the embodied souls of an individual and, with proper incorporation of sensible sparks of the energy, which forms the basis of life in this world.[8]

Divine master is the source of creation and ultimately all the creations diffuse in the supreme source. In that sense we can say that the Divine master is the source of the entire creation, and it diffuses once again at the ultimate moment to the source from which it diverged out[9].

Persons who cannot advance, or may experience some sort of obstacle in the path of knowledge, are pinted out in the Holy Scripture: those ignorant of true knowledge, those who lazily follow their animal or bemonic nature though capable of knowing the Divine, those inflected primarily with deluded intellect, and those with a demon like attitude and apprehensions.[10] Chapter 7 of the Bhagavadgita entirely narrates the true quality of a person who aspires for gaining knowledge for establishing oneself in the path of Jnana Yoga with proper affinity towards feeling the omnipresence of the Divine master, that person may then worship any of the idol or any of the cosmic form to feel the presence of such Divine spark within the self. That state of knowledge is the ultimate destiny towards which all the individuals are actually progressively and continuously advancing. Some of them are relying primarily on knowledge, some others take the support of knowledge foor performing with enhanced efficiency and some other, along with a bit deviation, refer surrendering oneself at the feet of the Divine master.

Advancement of all of such kinds are finally free to locate themselves in the broader realm of creations alongwith the waves of further manifestation of their individual soul some sort of higher purposes of life. Life of such kind impregnated primarily with divinity is the ultimate goal of life.

[1] Flood, Gavin (1996), An Introduction to Hinduism, Cambridge: Cambridge University Press, ISBN 0-521-43878-0

[2] [a] Ravi Dykema (2011). Yoga for Fitness and Wellness. Cengage. pp. 10–11. ISBN 978-0-8400-4811-0.;

[b] Orlando O. Espín; James B. Nickoloff (2007). An Introductory Dictionary of Theology and Religious Studies. Liturgical Press. p. 676. ISBN 978-0-8146-5856-7.;

[c] John M. Rector (2014). The Objectification Spectrum. Oxford University Press. pp. 198–201. ISBN 978-0-19-935542-6.

[3] Matilal, Bimal Krishna (2005), "Jnana", in Jones, Lindsay (ed.), MacMillan Encyclopedia of Religions, MacMillan

[4] Jones, Constance; Ryan, James D., eds. (2006), Encyclopedia of Hinduism, Infobase Publishing

[5] M. V. Nadkarni (2016). The Bhagavad-Gita for the Modern Reader: History, interpretations and philosophy. Taylor & Francis. pp. 45–46. ISBN 978-1-315-43898-6.

[6] J.J. Chambliss (2013). Philosophy of Education: An Encyclopedia. Routledge. p. 271. ISBN 978-1-136-51168-4.

[7] Robert W. Roeser (2005), An introduction to Hindu Indiaís contemplative psychological perspectives on motivation, self, and development, in M.L. Maehr & S. Karabenick (Eds.), Advances in Motivation and Achievement, Volume 14: Religion and Motivation, Amsterdam: Elsevier, ISBN 978-07623-12-597, pp 305-308

[8] The Bhagavadgita (VII -5)

[9] The Bhagavadgita (VII – 6)

[10] The Bhagavadgita (VII – 15)

CHAPTER TWENTY-THREE

Purushottam Yoga

The Purushottam Yoga, as vividly narrated by Saga Vyasa in Chapter 15 of the Bhagavadgita, signifies the quality and aspirations depending upon which an individual can feel the ascent of the soul towards harnessing the desired omnipresence of the Divine. It also enshrines the quality with which such person can move on throough the path of spirituality for feeling oneself being enlightened.

A true worshipper of knowledge having devotion to the Divine master can move successfully without much obstacle towards the supreme lord and it leads the individual ultimately to renunciation. That Divine world, having enough potential of offering liberation to a soul, is not illuminated or exhibited by solar, lunar or any other illuminations of any luminous or non-luminous objects of any form.[1]

We are in no doubt about the solution of an individual or a community as they were facing series of problems of varying degrees and of varying contexts. If we work out the relevance of the systematic teachings delivered by Sage Vyasa through the holy text then also it will become evident that Arjun has become a mere symbol of egoistic individual of society having some definite roles to play. Confusion regarding delivering duties often mounts their intellect and bring the state of crippleness in both sense organs and action organs duly restricted under the regulation of the umbrella of the EGO. Such a state of mind having a shadow of falsehood and EGO should be removed for redefining the role of that individual along with some concrete decisiveness in society.

Bhagavadgita represented such kind of effort of actualising the role of a person in the immediate surrounding. It was also conferred by the Divine power that oneness of the creation and the reator should be acknowledged by all of us to aspire for a collective progress.

The Holy Scripture also confers that we should make ourselves ready to admit that "Truth" is everywhere and cannot be the subject of our sole apprehension; we, along with some technological and spiritual advancement of markable ranks, started looking at other religions and philosophies for tracing out the accommodation of truth and non-violence. Such kind of convergance of spiritual initiative was at its beginning during the "Epic Age" as Sage Vyasa started such effort to configure the common markable teachings from Sankhya of Kapil Muni, Vedanta of holy Saints and Yoga of Sage Vashishtha and Sage Patanjali. It was, in that context of an effort of spiritual convergence, considered as a brilliant and time tested creation which may not lose the desired relevance even in near future. Such a claim is nat in blank as we are witnessing the involvement of a poet from Europe who has exhibited his caliber in translting the Holy Scripture of The Bhagavadgita in English without losing the poetic tune of the script.

Our motive force also drives us in the way duly inflicted with an aspiration of bringing out the grace of Holy Scripture to advocate the way people of Epic Age were addressing different social, political and religious problems of varying types. The Bhgavadgita will, without much deviation from the Vedic Doctrines of Indian origin, indicate precisely and convergantly the spirit in which we approach Peace and Non-violence and what exactly we aspire followers and devotees may derive from it prior to address any sort of problems duly, or in near future might develop, in society.

Reliance upon the Holy Text will increase day by day as it has enormous power of accommodating thought process springing out from other faculties of Yoga and Spirituality. The brilliant translation work of Sir. E. Arnold signifies such possibilities with greater degree of adherence towards the integration of human aspirations with the Holy Scripture of the Vedic Age.

[1] Bhagavadgita (XV – 6)

Approaches Of Convergence

Regarding doctrines of Nonviolence we must maintain our mind-set in such a way that it should not be judged from the angle of violence. From the view point of the regulation of senses Nonviolence (AHIMSA) is a state of mind which ensures the realm of our relations which distinguishes other human beings as relatives, strangers, friend, enemy or any other entity. Nonviolence will finalise the demarcation line within which our relatives gain some special treatment. Such kind of sense charged with the ritual of Nonviolence can consider a number of individuals as family members. With highest degree of such ritual filled with Nonviolence the individual start considering animals with care and respect. Animals are well treated in the family having higher state of Nonviolence as a ritual. In that context, with clear identification of the age old ritual, we can say that Nonviolence is the highest pursuit of socialisation and acculturation in a community. We cannot, even at any instance we should not, restrict the doctrine of Nonviolence to a limited quarter of any religious or social teachings. We should make it widely acceptable ritual irrespective of any social, cultural, physical or any geographical boundary. Restricting beauty of this ritual due to any reason is also a sin.

There are instances during which we gain several common resources from the nature. We are also getting equally exposed to global problems like pollution, depletion of ozone layers, war, cross border terrorism and many other problems. We are also getting exposed to the globally developed economic crisis due to various reasons. World Economic Forum formulated a list of most pressing points to be considered jointly to address majority of global problems (better we say it as issue).[1] These were: Food security, Inclusive growth, Future of work/unemployment, Climate change, financial crisis of 2007–2008, Future of the internet/Fourth Industrial Revolution, Gender equality, Global trade and investment and regulatory frameworks Long-term investment/Investment strategy and Future healthcare. It is also suggested that no single issue can be isolated or analysed individually at any instance. All the issues as incorporated in the list are directly or indirectly influenced by states of Peace and Nonviolence. The reason is very simple: Peace and Nonviolence signify the spiritual, mental and emotional set up of an individual. We all are, in that context, in the state of such situation where our alignment towards Peace and Nonviolence will be quantified.

The Core of Philosophy

From the context of Samkhya[2] Philosophy[3] it can be ascribed with utmost clarity that our entire set of mind and intellect are equally guided by the Ego. This concept, being most scientific, signifies creation of an individual due to interaction of two top most components (TATWA) namely Purusha[4] and Prakriti. Prakriti, being the direct participatory component of creation, includes all the cognitive, moral, psychological, emotional, sensorial and physical aspects of reality. Only Prakriti[5] acts under the orientation provided by another non-participant component namely "Purush" (it cannot be compared with electromagnetic or sub-atomic entity of driving forces or energy). Just below the sensible soul resides the pair of functional entity namely "mind" and "intellect". These paired entities are equally responsible for issuing functional command of different types for Ego (AHAM). It also signifies the quality with which the Ego will receive timely guidance. We can also bring change in the guidance issued to Ego by bringing some sort of alteration in the knowledge base and instructional mechanism. Quality parameter with which Ego works will also signify the quality of personality that the individual holds. Saints coined three different parameters with which quality of Ego can be standardized. It may be combination of best (extremely good), better (moderate) and worst (extreme bad) Ego. Combination of all the three qualities will make the personality as a unit. None of the segments will become absolute in combination and none of the quality units will be left out during formulation of the individual's consent.

Being part of an absolute consciousness, Purusha remains free from the creation unit and also remains free from any kind of quality distinction. It also remains pure and non-attributive.[6] This Ego will finalise the consent of human memory and intellect for qualifying or disqualifying any other entity of the surrounding as relative, friend or enemy. Such kind of class distinction duly made by the individual will finalise the pattern of treatment issued to different segments of society. If zone of family feeling is small then it is obvious that number of relatives will be least in number. Accordingly the human nature will be defined.

A Strategic Alignment

We often come across doctrines of Peace and Nonviolence from different sources of academics and spiritual realms. All sections of such kinds of spiritual settings and academics maintain some sort of identical notions regarding nature of these rituals. Difference to some extent can be identified in the form of approach of seeing these things from two extreme opposite poles. One can consider nonviolence from the angles of violence. Some other person having some higher spiritual enrichment can consider nonviolence from the angle of the spiritual refinement and modification of the quality parameters of Ego.[7] Whenever we start considering "Peace" as a doctrine of community living then it always appear along with the doctrine of "Nonviolence". The master of Yoga Philosophy proposed Nonviolence as one of the ritual under the coin "Yama"[8]. Here also we are witnessing presence of Ahimsa (Nonviolence) and truth (Satya)[9] as the essential mental state with which an individual attains some sort of enhancement in terms of quality of Ego needed for regulating other actions and performances of sensory, mixed as well as motor[10] impulses. Regulation of all such impulses will signify the personality scale with which the individual may remain active in the surrounding.

Different schools of Spirituality and religion may address these rituals differently, but principle at the core remains unalterable. We must feel the presence of divine besides us during all instances. It is the ultimate goal of a life. People start considering some of the acts and conducts according to their state of knowledge and span of information duly accommodated in mind. Along with such kind of mental and intellectual orientation an individual gains some sort of functional quality. Such individual also start searching other likeminded people having some sort of identical mental and intellectual set up of desired types. Gradual convergence of similar kind of mental and intellectually accustomed minds will form a commune. Such commune may gain an identity in the surrounding. Here takes birth a class, a community, a religious group, an organisation etc. If we aspire for attainment of unity and harmony of some wider types then it must move on through culmination of the status of mental and intellectual bases of varying types. Such kind of culmination will move on through converging approaches of the process of acculturation. It is also true that any kind of abrupt alteration may not be accepted by the members of diverged groups of community. They have some other guidelines issued from some other distant nuclear centre of socialisation and spiritual alignments.

There is another option through which spiritual convergence can be materialized. Community members should have a common core of state sponsored acculturation duly impregnated with principles of the spiritual, mental and intellectual core. In accord to the status we have, principally at the juncture of the Information age, a state sponsored acculturation which will move on smoothly and softly through participatory approaches by accommodating ideals, doctrines, rituals and principles. This approach will be populated gradually by integrating cultural differences of various stake holders of a society.

[1] Hutt, Rosamond (21 January 2016). "What are the 10 biggest global challenges?". World Economic Forum. Retrieved 18 January 2018.

[2] The word Samkhya means empirical or relating to numbers. Philosophy got its name Samkhya due to consideration of number of elements responsible for making creations possible. 25 true principles take part to ensure manifestation of a living being.

Reference: Apte, Vaman Shivaram (1957). The practical Sanskrit-English dictionary. Poona: Prasad Prakashan.

[3] Systematic enumeration and rational examination of an individual on the basis of the culmination of matter and energy to ensure creation.

Reference: Mikel Burley (2012), Classical Samkhya and Yoga - An Indian Metaphysics of Experience, Routledge, ISBN 978-0415648875, pages 47-48

[4] The creator element which influences the creation but never takes part physically in the process of creation.

[5] Lusthaus, Dan (2018), Samkhya, acmuller.net, Resources for East Asian Language and Thought, Musashino University

[6] Being non-attributive part of the creator power, Purusha remains off the quality parameters and also maintains its pure status. Reference: Sharma, C. (1997), A Critical Survey of Indian Philosophy, New Delhi: Motilal Banarsidass Publ, ISBN 81-208-0365-5

[7] There are three distinct parameters with which we signify quality of Ego: Extreme positive, extreme neutral and moderate types.

[8] Yama is the word coined by Sage Patanjali for accommodating five basic rituals (observable human activities) to make the individual fit for considering rules of spiritual living. These are AHIMSA (Nonviolence), SATYA (Truth), ASTEYA (Considering existence of Divine power as true), BRHMACHARYA (putting effort for attainment of knowledge) and APARIGRAHA (non-attachment to worldly existing things and not to store belongings in plenty).

Reference: Yogasutras (Theory of Yoga) by Sage Patanjali.

[9] David Kalupahana (1995), Ethics in Early Buddhism, University of Hawaii Press, ISBN 978-0824817022, page 8, Quote: The rational argument is identified with the method of Samkhya, a rationalist school, upholding the view that "nothing comes out of nothing" or that "being cannot be non-being".

[10] Impulse which gives motility and functional readiness to sense organs and action organs.

The Divine

Yoga is a science of living, a strategy of linking up the soul with the supreme master, a process of acknowledging the Divine omnipresence, a system of reviving coordination between different organ system, a sharp impetus of integrating spiritual and intellectual segment of the individual meant primarily for gaining ascent in the path of attainment of Divinity. Science of Yoga is widely discussed at different instances in Vedic Scriptures and Epics. All the treasure of olden times are not there in our hand; even some of the scriptures are partially interpreted; even some of the sources are differently interpreted; some of the scholarly discussions like that of Sage Kapil, Sage Patanjali, Sage Shankara etc. moved on differently to enrich Central Dogma of the Science of Yoga and Meditation.

Meditation is a kind of guided practice during which spiritual enrichment, mental clearness and emotional calmness will be the desired attainable state for which aspirants remain involved in the process.[1] Although it is evident from various schools of religion, then also guided practices of meditations are prominently placed in Vedantic Schools of religion, Jainism and Buddhism.[2] A clear distinction between soul and mind is the special approach and uniqueness of Vedantic traditions. It also confers the possibly of advancement for all the beings: [Purnamadah Purnamidan........][3]. Words inscribed in Veda, Upanishads and Epics are not merely words; stories are not merely stories; Verses are not merely any scholarly discourses; all such presentations convey the principal objective of making people (fellow aspirants) aware of the presence of the Divine besides their immediate context. The science of Meditation has some other applications too: it can reduce stress, anxiety, depression and pain during certain instances.[4] Exact translation of Dhyana is not exactly meditation; a limitation is there in between thought process of two extremes; contemplating upon some subject, thinking deeply, pondering upon something etc. are the scope of meditation. "Dhyana" and "Pranayaama" confer withdrawal of senses from the physical world, diverting all the senses towards the inner world of fellow aspirant, converging different sections of the wandering mind, regulation of breathing and impulse for attaining calmness of mind and diffusion of passion, regulating mind to let the illumination of soul become prominent. It is clear from the fact that we must not restrict the brightness of Dhyana and Pranayaam simply by using the term "Meditation." We also remain conscious while using "Dhyana" merely for attaining some success in terms of medical or physical means. Even aspirations of fellow individual should not be restricted to the progress of body parts and impulse transmission; it should have enough capabilities to ensure enhancement of the spiritual status of the being with which omnipresence of the Divine can be acknowledged. Such acknowledgement is also not the ultimate goal of Dhyana and Pranayaam; it is the juncture during which senses are diverted from externally sensible world to internally recognisable illuminations of soul; the power which guides mind and intellect; indirectly guides senses and organ system; perfectly works to ensure manifestation of finest particles.

A child from remote area of Bengal started visiting nearby primary school to take part in formal schooing. Teacher of that school (during early decades of 19th Century) was quite friendly; even the learning environment of that school was equally friendly. The fellow learner started learning basic mathematical operations. Lessons of adding numbers developed an impression of adding living forms (Jeevatma) and Supreme master (Paramatma). That phase of learning went on continuing up to a couple of months. Finally the curriculum of subtraction was to follow during forthcoming sessions; the fellow learner refused to join that session as he was spiritually not ready to tolerate the removal of Jeevatma (living forms) from the collections of the supreme master (the Paramatma); as the fellow learner was not ready to tolerate the removal of spiritual ascent from the soul; as the fellow learner was not ready to establish a halt in his progressive trend of spiritual ascent; as he wanted to recognise the Divine omnipresence at all instances of life. Due to such kinds of spiritual orientation of the fellow aspirant during childhood he left formal school and continued joining worships of different types duly organised by villagers at different places. His affinity towards the divine and his abled narrations related to supreme master often reflected onset of Divine ascent in the fellow individual at the tender age. Similar the situation was there during stages when Sage Shankaracharya preferred renouncing the world for spreading messages of spirituality.

There are several other examples displaying stages and instances of renunciation which made aspirants famous in due course of time. Sage Shankaracharya (an 8th Century Vedic Scholar and saint) presented a harmonizing reading of the sastras, with liberating knowledge of the self at its core, synthesizing the Advaita Vedanta[5] teachings of his time; about

300 additional texts were attributed to him afterwards.[6] His contributions like Brahmasutrabhashya, commentaries on The Bhagavadgita and ten principal Upanishads.[7] Advaita Vedanta was the principal contribution duly made by sage Shankara.[8] Sage Shankara (alternatively Adi Guru Shankaracharya) was in the forefront for reviving Vedic traditions during tenure of Chandragupta II Vikramaditya).[9] Some of the stotra (poetic works), the Daksinamurti Stotra, the Bhajagovinda Stotra, the Sivanandalahari, the Carpata-panjarika, the Visnu-satpadi, the Harimide, the Dasa-shloki, and the Krishna-staka are contributed by Sage Shankaracharya during that context.[10]

Saints from Indian context always worked differently to point out spiritual enrichment of Scriptures and Epics with which ascent in the path of Spirituality can be ensured. While introducing himself to his spiritual master for the first time Sage Shankara started narrating his real nature in the form of "Nirvanashatakam: I am Consciousness, I am Bliss, I am Shiva, I am Shiva ... " [11]. Advaita Veda, which existed before the saintly scholar, was actually systematised by him.[12] Monistic spirituality reflected periodically in his works; it was a shift from realism to idealism; a doctrine which ensured chances of indivual progress up to the identity of sureme master; a task of spiritual ascent which was acknowledged by the saint a possible and accomplishable destiny; a destiny which confers the regulation of senses, withdraw of senses from sensible objects, attainment of Divine knowledge; a competence which will ensure Divine omnipresence at the individual level.[13]

Understanding Brahman

Brahman, a supreme indestructible entity having enough capability of ensuring all sorts of worldly manifestations, is the masterly guide of the self (Adhyatma) and also plays a role in actions pertaining to the material personality of living beings, and its development (Karma). [14] Lord of sacrifices (Adhiyajna) resides in all individuals; masterly guide of all such individuals is the universal Divine (Adhidaiva) and ever-continuing manifestations and alterations of worldly manifestations (Adhibhuta) makes the world a reality. Aspirants having capability of sustaining Dhyana to the Divine subject gains liberation; such contemplation provides them similar kinds of awareness; such kind of absolute involvement of the fellow aspirant in Divine subject by mind and intellect will undoubtedly provide them opportunities of recognising the Divine omnipresence; such awareness will facilitate the fellow individual in recognising the Divine as the Supreme creator, absolute source from which rest of the other manifestation become a reality; it is the omniscient(the most ancient); the possessor of an inconceivable divine form; stays beyond all darkness of ignorance; is brighter than brightness of the sun; is recognisable by fixing life –ignition (Prana) between the eyebrows and steadily remembering presence of the supreme master in all forms of creations. Great ascetics practice the vow of celibacy regularly and renounce worldly pleasures to gain the proximity to the imperishable one (the Divine). One can establish the self in steadfast yogic concentration by restraining all the gates of the body and fixing the mind in the heart region, and then drawing the life-breath to the head. While chanting "OM" (the Prabava) aspirants attain the supreme goal by overcoming bodily obstacles. Aspirants fixing on the Divine subjects with utter devotion recognises the masterly guide at all instances, and by doing so regularly they overcome the fear of turbulent cycle birth and death; as they readily attain the highest order of perfection in life. [15]

Up to the highest abode of the supreme Divine, for which we have little instances of sensible recognitions, for which we have some imaginary impetus, for which we ascribe several theories and propositions while relying upon the nature of manifestations duly accomplished, for which organisms will be subject to creation and destruction. Aspirants relying on the supreme master remain free from the fear of birth and death. One day of Brahma (kalp) lasts a thousand cycles of the four ages (mahā yug) and his night also extends for the same duration. One can understand the real nature of night and day in a broader spectrum; our earthly limitations of days and nights are restricted only up to the horizons of atmosphere; beyond the scope of atmosphere solar radiations start traveling ceaselessly towards the outer world. Light start travelling ceaselessly in a straight path in the Universe and start creating sense of vision by striking any non-luminous objects and bouncing off the surface of that object; in that context brightness and visibility of the Moon may change but that of the Sun remain unaltrerable for considerable time interval. Creation and destruction of the entire collection of worldly objects will indicate a day and night of Brahman.[16] There exists another dimensions of such kinds of cycles of creation and destruction inside the individual's soul which is often persist even after disintegration of all kinds of organ and system and collapse of all the senses. Unmanifested dimension of soul (Atma) is the final attainable goal (supreme abode of the Divine master), and upon reaching the same destiny, aspirants may not return to the worldly sensible desires and passion of the world. That supreme Divine is greater than all kinds of creations which physically exist as sensible and materially recognisable; the masterly creator of all sorts of worldly manifestations; a binding force which is active inside the centrally placed mass of an atom and also active at the farthest realm of the clusters of Galaxy. Those who know the Supreme Brahman and who depart from this world, during the six months of the sun's northern course, the bright lunar fortnight, and the bright part of the solar day, attain the desired supreme destination. The practitioners of Vedic rituals, who pass away during the six months of the sun's southern course, the dark fortnight of the moon, the time of smoke, the night, attain the celestial abodes. After enjoying celestial pleasures, they again return to the worldly manifestations. These two, bright and dark paths, always exist in this world and remain restricted at the realm of the Earth; other planets have their own instances of days and nights. The way of light leads to liberation and the way of darkness leads to recycling of the Divine manifestations. [17]

Aspirants having proper knowledge of the progression through the path of spirituality never get confused of worldly manifestations and after recognising the secret of all kinds of manifestations they gain merits superior than fruits attainable because of following Vedic rituals; following performance of sacrifice; by doing austerities and charities; by following masterly instruction of the spiritual master; by analysing real nature of the imperishable Atma (the Soul force); by acknowledging presence of the Brahman besides all kinds of worldly manifestations. [18]

Moksha, the liberation from sufferings and rebirth, is attained through illusoriness of the phenomenal world (as seems manifested because of the presence of Brahman) and disidentification from the body-mind complex and the notion of 'doership' (A creator or motivator of any of the activities duly regulated by the nature), and acquiring vidyā (knowledge) of one's true identity as Atman-Brahman (alternatively Soul force), self-luminous (svayam prakāśa[19]) awareness or consciousness which can be witnessed by the self.[20] Upanishadic statements such as tat tvam asi [21], destroy the ignorance or illusive intellect (avidyā) regarding one's true identity by revealing that (soul of living forms) Ātman is non-different from immortal accumulation of the supreme master (Paramatma). Adwaita Vedanta also elaborates preparatory practice on the basis of noble sayings (Mahavakyas) aiming ultimately towards attainment of liberation from confutions, sensory turbulence of contrasting feelings; such as distinction of happiness and sorrow, gains and loss, right and wrong, anger and passion; it also provides an ample scope of progress to individuals with which the fellow aspirant start recognising presence of the Divine creator besides all sorts of worldly manifestations.[22] Brahman is the true Self, consciousness, awareness, and the only Reality.[23]

[1] Jevning, R.; Wallace, R.K.; Beidebach, M. (September 1992). "The physiology of meditation: A review. A wakeful hypometabolic integrated response". Neuroscience & Biobehavioral Reviews. 16 (3): 415–424. doi:10.1016/s0149-7634(05)80210-6. PMID 1528528. S2CID 2650109.

[2] Dhavamony, Mariasusai (1982). Classical Hinduism. Università Gregoriana Editrice. p. 243. ISBN 978-88-7652-482-0. Archived from the original on 2023-03-17. Retrieved 2020-10-27.

[3] Om Puurnnam-Adah Puurnnam-Idam Puurnnaat-Puurnnam-Udacyate |

Puurnnasya Puurnnam-Aadaaya Puurnnam-Eva-Avashissyate ||

Om Shaantih Shaantih Shaantih ||

Meaning: Om, That (The Supreme Divine) is Purna (filled completely with Divine Consciousness); This (Inner Soul) is also Purna (filled with Divine Consciousness); Purna is manifested From Purna (From the Fullness of Divine Consciousness the complete sensible world is manifested). After taking Purna from the supreme source of Purna, Purna indeed remains (Because Divine Consciousness is Non-Dual, beyond the scope of distinctions of qualities and Infinite).

[4] Hölzel, Britta K.; Lazar, Sara W.; Gard, Tim; Schuman-Olivier, Zev; Vago, David R.; Ott, Ulrich (November 2011). "How Does Mindfulness Meditation Work? Proposing Mechanisms of Action From a Conceptual and Neural Perspective". Perspectives on Psychological Science: A Journal of the Association for Psychological Science. 6 (6): 537–559. doi:10.1177/1745691611419671. ISSN 1745-6916. PMID 26168376. S2CID 2218023. Archived from the original on 2020-10-02. Retrieved 2020-09-30.

[5] Non-duality of the Vedantic Doctrines.

[6] Hacker, Paul (1995), Halbfass, Wilhelm (ed.), Philology and Confrontation: Paul Hacker on Traditional and Modern Vedanta, SUNY Press, ISBN 978-0-7914-2582-4

[7] Mayeda, Sengaku (2006). A thousand teachings : the Upadeśasāhasrī of Śaṅkara. Motilal Banarsidass. ISBN 978-81-208-2771-4.

[8] Comans, Michael (2000), The Method of Early Advaita Vedānta: A Study of Gauḍapāda, Śaṅkara, Sureśvara, and Padmapāda, Delhi: Motilal

Banarsidass

[9] K.A. Nilakantha Sastry, A History of South India, 4th ed., Oxford University Press, Madras, 1976.

[10] Isaeva, Natalia (1993). Shankara and Indian Philosophy. Albany: State University of New York Press (SUNY). ISBN 978-0-7914-1281-7.

[11] Original Sanskrit: Nirvanashtakam Sringeri Vidya Bharati Foundation (2012);

English Translation 1: K Parappaḷḷi and CNN Nair (2002), Saankarasaagaram, Bhartiya Vidya Bhavan, ISBN 978-81-7276-268-1, pp. 58–59;

English Translation 2: Igor Kononenko (2010), Teachers of Wisdom, ISBN 978-1-4349-9898-9, p. 148;

English Translation 3: Nirvana Shatakam Isha Foundation (2011); Includes translation, transliteration and audio.

[12] Nakamura, Hajime (2004) [1950], A History of Early Vedanta Philosophy. Part Two, Delhi: Motilal Banarsidass Publishers

[13] Sharma, B.N. Krishnamurti (2000). History of the Dvaita School of Vedānta and Its Literature: From the Earliest Beginnings to Our Own Times. Motilal Banarsidass Publishers. ISBN 978-81-208-1575-9.

[14] The Bhagavadgita VIII. 3

[15] The Bhagavadgita VIII. 4 – 14.

[16] Discovery of Black Hole indicates the ever – continuing cycle of creation and destruction.

[17] The Bhagavadgita VIII. 16-26.

[18] The Bhagavadgita VIII. 27-28.

[19] Illuminating oneself without relying on any of the physical factors or biochemical regulators;

[20] Lipner, Julius (2000), "The Self of Being and the Being of Self: Samkara on "That You Are" (Tat Tvam Asi)", in Malkovsky, Bradley J. (ed.), New Perspectives on Advaita Vedānta, BRILL

[21] Translated as: "that['s how] you are,"

[22] Barua, Ankur (2015), "Ideas of Liberation in Medieval Advaita Vedānta", Religion Compass, 9 (8): 262–271, doi:10.1111/rec3.12160

[23] Potter, Karl H. (2008), Encyclopedia of Indian Philosophies Vol. 3: Advaita Vedānta Up to Śaṃkara and His Pupils, Delhi: Motilal Banarsidass Publishers, ISBN 978-81-208-0310-7

Collective Progress

We will now focus on the efforts with which congress of people's aspiration can be made possible to replace all sorts of patchy repairs by incorporating desired level of linkages at the dynamics of groups, community, society and individuals. Individual may move on to fulfil basic needs of the immediate family members first. After fulfilling such needs they start considering needs of other community members of the immediate surroundings. Such kind of political, social or spiritual nexus will finally make the entire community bonded with the impetus of sharing and caring. We will gradually witness development of community level network of sharing and caring on the basis of contemplated wishes and willingness of varying degree and of varying impetus. Here comes the situation when we may witness presence or absence of some sort of mental and intellectual status of community members duly impregnated with peace and Non-violence. We will also witness development of some higher bands of spiritual union which can finally play a vital role in spreading the doctrines of peace and nonviolence at the greater degree duly aligned positively with community consciousness.

Efforts of such kind of collective execution will also raise the level of confidence of other community units and they also come up with higher aspirations of joining hands to make the development of unified human efforts of enhanced spirituality standards a reality. People start considering the doctrines of peace and nonviolence after keeping themselves free from crippled apprehension of some small purposes of life. They also start safeguarding wills and wishes of the other community members and start helping each other collectively to cast off their affinity towards acts of animism[1]. Animism is also considered as one of the Anthropological concept of earlier times and is not the first one.[2] It also maintains its concern with the fact related to the unit which is alive and the factors which keep the unit alive.[3] An old concept of this Animism maintains a distinct idea depending upon which animals or some other non-human living entities were considered as a living unit which cannot understand differences between matter and life.[4] Animism was finally seen as an error or mistake due to which different schools of religion grew (Edward B. Tylor). They even started maintaining some sort of distinct identity of their own.[5] We should therefore continue working on this issue until and unless the perpetual unity of desired types is properly maintained. Our awareness and mutual conduct will also start taking a definite shape after inculcating cultural, spiritual and technological apprehensions of people of immediate surroundings. Threat to humanity in and around our society is enormous. Some of the threat can be addressed simply by making community aware of their duty and rights in a society. We also confer establishment of a balance between rights and duties through which aspirations of an individual in a society is advanced.

Progressive Human Bonds

Progress of the expansion of human bonds for materializing special conducts on the basis of the doctrines of peace and nonviolence will definitely contemplate a new horizon through which Inter-cultural citizenship bands can be made possible. We also exercise the process of bringing intellectual union amongst the participant members of community with which the networked information transfer and sharing of ideals will become easy as well as confluent one. We will even contingent to certain extent for making our effort a result oriented one by letting participation of distant community member possible in the joint efforts duly planned and implemented by members of the closed user groups. One should rely perpetually on the efforts of dialogues, discussion and progressive efforts of welfare for cultivating the possibilities of making people united by all means. It is also true that this effort of linking people on the basis of peace and nonviolence may not be an initiative of one sided impetus. People working on this process will definitely exercise mechanisms of inculcating the doctrines of peace and nonviolence without becoming influenced by the prejudice and bias. Peace and nonviolence may not be considered as any identifiable entity in nature without addressing involvement of any socially and spiritually oriented individuals residing the closed quarter under consideration duly inflicted with family feelings.

Community Experimentation

Is there any finishing line in the path of community experimentation? Do we expect some new dimensions in our community experimentations in relation to time? How do different gaps (such as gender gap, information gap, knowledge gap, gap of accessibility to resources, gap of spiritual alignments etc.) will be addressed through community experimentation?

Our understanding and approach will definitely permit us to consider all the above issues as per the convenience of approaches and resource utilisation. None of the community members should be left behind. If anyone or any group of individuals remains off the main stream then they may create a reverse current through which swiftness of collective progress will be hampered. Both Mahatma and Vinba[6] were aware of this fact and due to that reason they proposed the mechanism of ANTYODAYA (starting incorporation of the effort of addressing problems of the poorest and marginalised ones with priority). It was the impetus which coined an opportunity for Joseph Cornelius (popularly called by mahatma "Kumarappa") to design the implements of "Peace Economy". Economic plan without incorporating aspirations of poor and marginalised will not bring any collective progress. Only collective progress will ensure multi-layered unity in between closed as well as distant communities. In that context also aspirations of poorest and marginalised ones should be addressed with priority. Finally to say community experimentation is the vast area having enormous potential. It can be addressed from different angles. All such angles (more than 14 specified sectors)[7] were identified by Mahatma and his fellow associates during the period of pre-independent India. Lanza del Vasto was another associate of Mahatma who worked a lot in the field of community experimentation and successfully assimilated spiritual alignment of Mahatma and Saint Vinoba through his service lines. Lanza used to accompany Mahatma during morning walk to gain the blissful interactions with absolute and clear apprehensions. He has successfully gained a momentum in his approaches through community experimentation. We came across a long distance while discussing approaches and willingness with which successors of Mahatma worked at different instances. Still we have miles to go until and unless the World Peace in its absolute sense is properly established. Individuals who continued following doctrines of development proposed by Mahatma and his associates preferred implying adequate focus on villages. They also maintained that bright future of a nation resides in the development of villages. Collective effort of such development will definitely ensure the parallel development of other entities linked to the network of villages. It is also confirmed from the plan proposals prepared by planners after attainment of independence that India moved off the track of the principles and proposals of Mahatma. Power continued remaining centralised without ensuring participation of the villagers in the networked planning process.

It is true that success of a government resides in the effective execution with which generals and officers engaged in the process of planning and implementation deliver their duties. Performance of individual resides in the process with which they continue delivering their duties while maintaining adequate coordination with other sectoral units of government. Executing of different units of government network resides in the knowledge base with which professionals involved in a process delivers duty.

This approach is perfectly focused on the attainment of true knowledge which will enable the individual to feel the omnipresence of the Divine. With such kind of knowledge assimilation that individual can even recognise the presence of the Divine in all other creations duly attained varying degrees and extents of manifestation. If such kind of alteration at the individual level goes on progressive then it is obvious that such kinds of individuals move forward to create extended human bonds.

Due to such kinds of enhanced awareness and structured approaches of further socialisation the value system will be protected by all means. Doctrines of Peace and Nonviolence can be addressed properly through such groups of people having affinity towards recognising the TRUTH, for such acts of recognition will actualise them all spiritually, for such acts of recognition will enable them to impart themselves in the ever continuing process of socialisation, for all such efforts designed on the basis of comprehensive doctrines of Peace and Nonviolence will be addressed perfectly. Personality development is also attains a base of social, intellectual and spiritual base upon which foundation stones of personality are laid.[8] Individuals also interpret contextual situation from different possible angles to develop an enduring pattern of personality trait.[9] Human beings continued developing cultural, spiritual, attitudinal and physiological modifications through prolonged ages of evolution.[10] Personality and individuality are also developed accordingly through ages.

Situation was rightly addressed by Sage Vyasa Muni to address instances of conflicts in the light of spiritual awakening of an individual for want of attaining perfect levels of confidence and will power to allocate the desirable in which one could address different types of problems, agony and discontentment for the purpose of offering services to the wise and also for issuing some sort of resistance to the culprits; for such kinds of approach will finalise the real culmination of knowledge and action for the purpose of bringing out a concrete stand amidst instances of conflicts.

Objective of the Gita is obviously cannot be restricted up to the small purpose of life; only to attain victory in battlefield, or merely to nullify instances of misfortune, or merely springing up in life on the basis of the discourses of yoga of Knowledge, Devotion or Actions(Karma). It provides a balanced way of living standard with which aspirants can feel the Divine omnipresence, can recognise the spark of the any segment of the same Divine in every creations, can recognise dos and don'ts of life, can perpetuate all sorts of understanding to attain completeness in life; a completeness just like that of the Divine Master.

[1] It is (Animism) often considered as the faith of some Indigenous people. One can even confer the development of such acts simply for fulfilling basic needs of life without remaining inflicted with any kind of Spiritual or intellectual ascent.

Reference: Hicks, David (2010). Ritual and Belief: Readings in the Anthropology of Religion (3 ed.). Roman Altamira. p. 359. Tylor's notion of animism—for him the first religion—included the assumption that early Homo sapiens had invested animals and plants with souls ...

[2] Bird-David, Nurit (1999). ""Animism" Revisited: Personhood, Environment, and Relational Epistemology". Current Anthropology. 40 (S1): S67. doi:10.1086/200061.

[3] Harvey, Graham (2005). Animism: Respecting the Living World. London: Hurst & Co. ISBN 978-0-231-13701-0.

[4] Harvey, Graham (2005). Animism: Respecting the Living World. London: Hurst & Co. ISBN 978-0-231-13701-0.

[5] Tylor, Edward Burnett (1871). Primitive Culture: Researches into the Development of Mythology, Philosophy, Religion, Art, and Custom. Vol. 1. J. Murray. p. 260.

[6] Acharya Vinoba Bhave was the Spiritual successor of Mahatma who also addressed constructive work programmes duly planned by Mahatma for making the entire effort successful.

He had also incorporated some spiritual alignment to the service lines in which fellow volunteers remained deeply linked up.

[7] Sectors specified by Mahatma are clearly mentioned in the Constructive Work Programmes suggested by his fellow associates.

[8] Cervone, Daniel; Shadel, William G.; Jencius, Simon (February 2001). "Social-Cognitive Theory of Personality Assessment". Personality and Social Psychology Review. 5 (1): 33–51. doi:10.1207/S15327957PSPR0501_3. ISSN

1088-8683. S2CID 16223943.

[9] Cervone, Daniel; Shadel, William G.; Jencius, Simon (February 2001). "Social-Cognitive Theory of Personality Assessment". *Personality and Social Psychology Review*. 5 (1): 33–51. doi:10.1207/S15327957PSPR0501_3. ISSN 1088-8683. S2CID 16223943.

[10] Bell, M. G. (2010, January 1). *Consciousness: The Evolution Of The Self And Personal Individuality*. Retrieved November 1, 2014, from www.agenthuman.com/product/
evolution_self_personal_individuality.html#selfevol

Scholars and saints collected different flowers from the garden of Upanishad to prepare a Holy Script of instructions for a fellow warrior to diffuse his states of illution as he was to face a large number of enemies amidst a battle field. Recognising the Divine and performing according to instructions duly issued by the supreme master to fellow aspirant is the real objective of a life form.

The Divine Manifestation

Upanishad rightly maintains views related to universal reality of the Divine; presence of the same at all instances of creations; one should recognise presence of such masterly guide besides all creations; by doing so one should not try to grab resources belonging to others.

Description: C:\Users\Web Hosting\Pictures\ish--1.png

Affinity to work actively for hundreds of years for betterment of society and humanity never puts the fellow aspirant in the bondage of works by any means. Individual who violates the verdict of Soul force finally move towards the world of utter darkness devoid of sources of illuminations.[1] A stationary entity which can move even faster than the mind, even non-accessible to Gods, for it remains frontwardly progressive; passes beyond the progressive aspirant whenever they move forward. Master of Life establishes waver of ether and water in that ever expanding zone of creations; that moves and even remains stationary, that is far and also besides all creations, remains both inside and outside of all the worldly manifestations. [2] All sorts of hatred and violence will be diffused if fellow aspirant start recognising presence of all manifestations in the Divine and can recognise Divine omnipresence in all kinds of manifestations. Person of such self luminous intellect, having a clear vision of recognising presence of Brahman (the Divine) in all instances of manifestations, remains free from agony, illution, greed and sorrow. [3]

Description: C:\Users\Web Hosting\Pictures\sha-8.jpg

"Person inflicted with illution comes under the confinement of darkness and individuals relying exclusively on knowledge remain trapped amidst more darkness; for only knowledge without judicious actions cannot bring knowledge in action; such bands of knowledge without effective action brings agony, develops sorrow and often puts aspirants in a state of confusion."[4]

Aspirant who recognises Truth as a combination of knowledge and illusion experiences death due to wrong deeds and also becomes famous due to assimilation of knowledge. Person exhibiting devotion to birth alone comes under the trap of utter darkness of illution and confusion. We receive something by birth and some other thing by non-birth; such thought process is transmitted to us from nobles. After recognising birth and dissolution of birth as identical process aspirants gain fame even after getting restricted due to regulations of death. [5]

Discussion implies that abosolute knowledge alone cannot bring fame, truth exists in the combination of illusive knowledge and true knowledge; aspirants are exposed equally to fame and death; fame alone cannot restrict an individual to escape regulations of death and birth. It also implies accessibility of individals to both fame and illusion and progress of the same towards attainment of Divinity while remaining under the abled guidance of any Divine master.

Ego [Aham]

Aham (alternatively Ego) is the regulator of senses and actions through mind and intellect and also acts under the three scale parameters of qualities (such as SATWA or good qualities, RAJAS or ignorance and TAMAS or animism). It can be shifted from one quality scale to the other during worldly manifestations of life; it cannot be diffused completely; even it cannot be made absolutely free from any of the quality scales; we cannot limit our efforts to guide all actions and knowledge assimilation merely on the basis of any one quality parameter.

The Ego acts in accord to reality principle.[6] Besides sense of the very self it includes psychic functions such as judgment, tolerance, reality testing, control, planning, defense, synthesis of information, intellectual functioning, and memory. It can be considered as an organisation principle upon which thoughts, propositions and interpretations of the world are based.[7] The self, as considered as a driving force of development and shifting of Ego from one quality to the other, is the culmination of several archetypes.[8] The self (along with embodiment of Ego) is the autonomous center of the psyche which also works as the principal source of dream and real life experiences; it (the Self) works as the authority figure in dreams.[9]

All the regulatory mechanism with which ego works is quite difficult to identify and categorise; we simply predict the probable reason with which ego often diverts differently to accomplish false-self organisation during various real life instances; such organisation can have poor knowledge base; some kind of ignorance related to self-advancement may play a definitive role during that moment; a kind of flase- notion may be the probale reason which directs ego to accomplish false-self organisation. There are some instnaces of such organisation: closure to health for supporting individual to regain normal health status by the true self; doing the same to support social behaviour, manners and courtesy; protects the unactualised true self; removes true self completely during severe conditions.[10] Ego of a parent, in case of general instances of parental cares evident in higher group of animals including human beings, has its back reference through which such behaviours are transmitted from one generation to the other; a trend of gradual ascent from humanism to animism can be observed in certain cases.[11]

***.

Science of Exploration

Wider dimensions and expanded coverage of the teachings of Gita often make people worried about what to follow and what not to follow in real life. Also in some cases it becomes difficult to think about propositions in the actual ground. Because of lack of timely relevant practical knowledge of the situation, people even keep themselves aside from following and internalising teachings of the holy book in the real life situation. Approach of such religious and cultural teaching, therefore, should have proper considerations of some practical aspects of rituals and worships.

Some people maintain a view regarding Gita is that the entire aspects depicted in this holy book are a confusing one. Saints from olden times worked differently to show that Gita is much relevant in terms of rituals and propositions presented in it. Here also we are trying to trace out a link up in between rituals, traditions and practices that we have in nature to reestablish the age old faiths of the omnipresence of divine within us at its varying formats.

We can see things as they occupy a definite shape. We cannot see energy and power due to their in capabilities of occupying space. To feel the presence of such powers in our surrounding, we often take the support of our senses and feelings. In some cases our observations are evidence based, in some other cases it may have some imaginary propositions. Here comes the act of limitations that restrict us to feel Ultraviolet and Infrared [12]radiations which remained off the band of the visible spectrum and duly restricted our sense of vision seven visible waves of light.

There arises another question related to our effort of analyzing the relevance of the teachings of The Gita in present day situation. It was the instructions delivered by Lord Krishna to Arjun during the epic age of Vedic Civilisation. That time war had its presence in the scope of royal management. That time conflicts had a final termination to war for making efforts a result oriented. Sins and sinners had their presence in olden times and are still there with us today; format and geo-locations might vary; arms and ammunitions might differ. Even from the pages of history we can see how Prince Ashoka smashed the Kingdom of Kalinga only because that kingdom had refused to hand-over the murderer of his mother to him. Later on the war and the loss of lives of many innocent people had implied a deep impression in his mind and he had decided to refuse to take part in any other battle simply meant for territorial expansion. Teachings of The Gita have worked differently during different instances of the development of conflicts and agony.

Since conflicts and agony are beyond the scope of any historic time line, we can correlate teachings of any instances to prepare strategic actions of any other present day sectoral management plans. It has the impetus of the absolute knowledge of human actions, wishes, wills and conducts with absolute apprehension of delivering the needful.

The reason of discontentment, sorrow and agony of Arjun after entering the battle field was rejected instantly by Lord Krishna through implying a sanction of his indulgence in the war. Killing any individual or creating another one is not the role of any warrior. A warrior can deliver the duty in time with a clear impetus of making the wiser side victorious. Sinners will lose their lives because of their mis-conducts only.

It is the right place to mention about Upanishads, often referred as Vedantas, as they exhibit doctrines, rituals and worship patters prevalent in later Vedic Civilisation.[13] Those rituals and doctrines were duly incorporated in the great epics to make all sorts of teachings easy to understand. The Bhagavadgita along with majority of Upanishads and Brahmasutra are known as PRASTHANATRAYEE.[14] These three scriptures were studied extensively time to time to inculcate more relevant knowledge related to Divinity and Spirituality. Out of 108 known texts of Uapnishads only a dozen from the initial collection are considered as Primary (MUKHYA).[15] Concluding parts of Brahmans and Aranyaks are also filled with Mukhya Upanishads.[16] Authorship of all the anonymous tests duly collected from the garden of Upanishads is unknown. Group of saints might have collected and represented their lessons in the form of a collection.[17] Conversation between women like Maitreyi and Gargi are also inscribed in the holy texts of Uanishads.[18] Root of all such creations is principally radiated out time to time in different forms and also in different sectorian units from Vedas.

Pluralism of world view was characterised by the Upanishadic age; gradually inclined more towards dualism by combining Sankhya and Yoga doctrines efficiently.[19] The Bhagavadgita moved on a step forward by incorporating Vedanta along with Upanishadic dcotrines with an aspirations of delivering a common pattern of rituals, social formats and political will to the youths of the olden times.

Maitri Upanishad aspires for attainment of reverence and completeness by human beings with the help of the knowledge of Brahmans and repeated practices of meditation on such knowledge by the self.[20]

Further study of the Bhagavadgita reveals all such studies like the gradual unfoldment of petals of a lotus.

In the modern world we have various types of cultural and religious thought process possessing rituals, customs and traditions of different types , which are equally competent to enrich people in terms of knowledge, devotion, courage, will power and dedication. The way we receive each culture to enrich our multiplurality will specify our degrees and ranges of success. Our motive force will guide accordingly to explore possibilities of working out converged cultural segments from all the rituals to move up towards vibrant waves of multi plurality.

India , at this juncture of the development of multiplurality, will be a best example for all of us. Here people learned a lot to live with each other, tolerate each other and enrich each other differently.

We cannot see light. Even we cannot see the propagation of sound through the material medium. Light strikes our eye, reaches our brain and develops a sensation of vision through certain life process of vision. With some sort of illusion, or lack of true knowledge only, we often claim that we can see light. Even all the colours radiated out from the sun are not recognisable by us. If God resides inside the individual, if all mysteries related to the ascent of a person on the path of divinity, then why any devotee search it out for gaining the blessings of any Divine power located outside the physically existing body? Why such a dwindling situation any individual face during the tenure of worship?

Lord Krishna narrated essence of feeling the Divine communion with the physically existing life through witnessing cultivation of knowledge, actualisation of the presence of any supreme power in sub conscious mind and possible ways and means to follow that power. It enables an individual to come across the feeling of the advent of some completeness in the mind through knowledge transformation. Cultivation of knowledge regarding the relationship of the divine and disciple is enrouted from the age old traditions through the turmoil of the organic evolution. That evolution brought some change in the process of exhibits, but the core remained the same. It was even more perpetual and more profound regarding the ability of harnessing the relationship of matter and energy. We cannot imagine the existence of matter without the involvement of energy, and similarly energy takes a definite visible form to occupy certain space in this universe.

How do people see things and how do they correlate such unavoidable relationship of energy and matter is depend upon the level of understanding that one adheres with. A master of Physics and a master of Phylosophy must have varying degree of explanations for putting forth the mystery behind the mechanism involved during inter-conversion of matter and energy. All organic combinations have certain physical and chemical sets of combinations in such a definite ways that they inculcate the abilities of interactions and abilities of giving birth to senses. Even evolution of sensory structures and related orientations became much collaborative in case of human beings. Here occurs a change which brought us near the state of explorations meant for examining the hidden mysteries behind creation and orientation of life forms in the living planet.

These days, things are known to us that earth like situation exists in the universe. Only the matter of concern is that we may not be able to reach the place even after attaining the speed as that of light in a year or two. Only we can admire the presence and orientation of such creations within our visibility. Only we can explore and examine such things with the help of optical and electronic instruments. With an understanding of such limitations human beings never arranged any voyage to explore the inner world of senses that can allow us to explore the outer orientation of time and space. Such an inner world exploration may require a little effort to culminate senses within a confinement for feeling the presence. There also resides a tremendous flux of energy accumulated within such a small space. Those mysterious combinations taking the form of life were explored differently by saints during olden times.

There developed a science of explorations of the correlations of the Creation and the Divine. Matter and energy indulged in a perfect orientation for letting senses flow through them. Arrangement and orientation of all our senses are directed outwardly. That is why we are bound to receive waves and sparks from the outside world. Our inner world remains unexplored in most of the cases. Only adherence of true knowledge and the journey of senses through inner world during meditation can pave a way out for exploring our own self. Meditation is the doorstep where orientation of senses get diverted towards the inner world and bring out mysteries associated to the fact of accommodation of the Divine power inside the living being.

Is that Divine power is restricted to the human beings only? The answer is, obviously and surely without any doubt, No. human beings has gained some sort of evolutionary supremacy in due course of time, but other beings are also of same potential and courage with a domination of animism in them. Dogs are loyal to their master, cats exhibit better vigilance power, elephants are more socialised beings having better memory power and tigers are the masters of their own territory. Taking hold upon the surrounding and defining the role according to trophic [21] level, we can easily arrange these beings and others without any difficulty.

Philosophical and Spiritual supremacy is a step forward that makes a distinction between other animals and human beings. Then also we can witness inhuman acts from human beings and humanly acts from some inhuman animals. The orientation of sense organ and correlation of senses and sensory responses with memory and intellect is the only factor regulating such varying degrees and conducts of animismic and hunmanismic behaviours.

Presence of such a Divine power within the creation is the reason behind the maintenance of an idea of serving humanity with a correlated apprehension of serving God. Only God cannot put a direct access to the feelings of the presence of such immense power within us. It is the approach with which we offer our services to living beings can develop a way out for us to feel the difference.

Once during pre-independent period in Bombay (at present Mumbai) a youth from some semi urban place approached a saint for offering himself at the service to divine. It made the saint happy. He wanted to know the exact reason behind his stand of doing so. Saint also enquired about his capabilities and considered his offering a wise one. Actually the fellow was searching jobs in the city. He was also a normal Graduate from any sub –urban area and his financial situation was also not so good. Perhaps the sacrifice might make him temporarily happy and contented, but will become a burden in due course of time. With happiness saint suggested him for searching out a suitable job and helping the parents and inmates of the family financially. Only After gaining some wealth and knowledge the person can really enjoy the glory of sacrifice. Right now the person has nothing special to sacrifice. Such sacrifice inflicted with sorrow and agony may put both the master and the disciple in trouble.

Even divine cannot allow any individual to put oneself and families in trouble and agony. It is the only state of contentment that helps a person during movement from the physical world to the spiritual world. Offerings of any kind and in any particular form will bring happiness.

Mind Vs Intellect

Learning even continued beyond the scope of interactive curriculum transaction with aspirations of enhancing critical skills and confidence of the active members of the society.

In simple words, we can say that the advanced Value system enabled people to understand and maintain their fundamental value system on the basis of the popular cultural and traditional base of olden times. For widening this type of practice with an aspiration of collective progress, people started sharing minute particulars of their feelings on any specified thing or propositions to keep the progressive trend active and to ascertain its ascending mode.

The gradual refinement in value system has come in the form of rituals and observations. In modern day context the human value system has a character of an exhibit of a convergence of differently developed value systems. The kind of convergence of both eastern and the western value system has enabled the development of Missionary Culture in the Indian context. Such missionary culture has enabled people to readjust their acts and conducts on the basis of some masterly instructions that they duly received through scheduled discourses of their masterly guide. None of such value system is entirely aligned towards the west and not even towards the Vedic culture. Combination and recombination of value system always reflect some sort of Yoga Philosophy with an affinity towards naming it differently for making oneself satisfied. Lord Buddha, for a simple example, has cultivated eight fold simple path of worship having a proposition identical to that of the Yoga Philosophy and acts and conducts duly proposed by Saint Patanjali. The path proposed by Lord Buddha became popular in some of the society due to advent of easiness in the worship.

The missionary culture in Bengal duly introduced by Shri Ramakrishna has the identical affinity of bringing the Yoga based acts and conducts to people with easiness. It has also designed a service oriented mechanism of worship based on the principle of "Serving Man, Serving the Divine." It has also gained success and brought its prominence through cultivating ideals of Saint Patanjali. Ramakrishna wanted people to keep faith on the presence of the Divine. As we cannot feel the presence of all kinds of waves of energy because of our limitations of senses, similarly we cannot feel the omnipresence of the supreme power within us because of our incapabilities of imbibing the waves of the supreme power. Only because of this reason we cannot deny the presence of such divine power within ourselves and within the others.

We can see things as they occupy a definite shape. We cannot see energy and power due to their in capabilities of occupying space. To feel the presence of such powers in our surrounding, we often take the support of our senses and feelings. In some cases our observations are evidence based, in some other cases it may have some imaginary propositions. Here comes the act of limitations that restrict us to feel Ultraviolet and Infrared radiations which remained off the band of the visible spectrum and duly restricted our sense of vision seven visible waves of light.

Once people of Kolkata wanted to judge the knowledge base of Saint Ramakrishna. A group of learned persons and veterans from the city visited the temple where Ramakrishna used to deliver his services by preying goddess Kali in his own language and also by claiming incidents of his conversation with Goddess Kali. The matter became very critical when Raasmani, the main patron of Ramakrishna, came to know about this incident. Inmates of the temple and the royal family wanted to work out any alternatives, but firmness of Ramakrishna made them more confident about the knowledge enrichment that the saint had.

People came in and took their respective seats within the small residential block of the fellow saint. His happiness and contentment exhibited his firmness and fearlessness. People prepared to throw questions towards him. With a gentle smile Ramakrishna described a narration in short, "Once an idol made of salt moved on to measure the depth and expansion of ocean. We all can easily imagine what happened to that idol. Returning back from his status became impossible. I have nothing more to say, now it's your turn. Ask me."

The kind of voice and firmness to face all sorts of questions made people worries about their own limit of knowledge. Ramakrishna had narrated an incident which was from Vedantic teachings. It made people confirmed about the knowledge enrichment of the saintly person having a common look with some uncommon adherence to the immediate divine. The judgement went on differently and some among them had accepted Ramakrishna as their true guide in their respective path of spiritual ascent.

Spirituality, in its true sense, should not put any individual off the track of society and culture. It should cultivate the essence of true knowledge for the purpose of the collective enrichment of the referred commune through making their overall spiritual ascent towards integral progress more and more confluous.

Instead of having all such knowledge of Veda, Epics and other spiritual worshipping mechanism, Ramakrishna preferred offering food to Goddess Kali in the way people offer to any other living beings. The kind of contentment itself exhibited his effort of linking people of some common living to their holy mother and immediate divine.

Most critical aspect that Saint Ramakrishna had to handle appeared in front of him in the form of Narendranath Dutta, later on popularly received the name Swami Vivekananda. Naren wanted to judge the actual claim of Ramakrishna regarding his conversation with the divine power. Repeatedly he started approaching his master and repeatedly started blaming him for his claim of enjoying divine communion as a false one. Ultimately the day came when the young Naren had something to beg during his divine communion. It was arranged by his master to nullify the doubts and confusion which was hampering the intellect of the young student of Philosophy. The conflict in the mind of Narendranath was going on due to his contradictory knowledge of Western and Eastern Philosophical ideas, due to his affinity of examining divine power with an intention of jotting down scientific evidences, due to his lack of true knowledge regarding non-avoidable coupling of matter and energy and due to his lack of faith in exploring the divine omnipresence in some incidents of immediate surroundings.

Depth and expansion of the knowledge is so enormous that we can simply feel it and try to acquire it by part on the basis of our capabilities, willingness and interests. Once people of Kolkata wanted to judge the knowledge base of Saint Ramakrishna. A group of learned persons and veterans from the city visited the temple where Ramakrishna used to deliver his services by preying goddess Kali in his own language and also by claiming incidents of his conversation with Goddess Kali. The matter became very critical when Rani Raasmani, the main patron of Ramakrishna, came to know about this incident. Inmates of the temple and the royal family wanted to work out any alternatives, but firmness of Ramakrishna made them more confident about the knowledge enrichment that the saint had.

People came in and took their respective seats within the small residential block of the fellow saint. His happiness and contentment exhibited his firmness and fearlessness. People prepared to throw questions towards him. With a gentle smile Ramakrishna described a narration in short, "Once an idol made of salt moved on to measure the depth and expansion of ocean. We all can easily imagine what happened to that idol! Returning back to his original status became impossible. I have nothing more to say, now it's your turn. Ask me whatever you want to ask."

The kind of voice and firmness to face all sorts of questions made people worries about their own limit of knowledge. Ramakrishna had narrated an incident which was from Vedantic teachings. It made people confirmed about the knowledge enrichment of the saintly person having a common look with some uncommon adherence to the immediate divine. The judgement went on differently and some among them had accepted Ramakrishna as their true guide in their respective path of spiritual ascent.

Spirituality, in its true sense, should not put any individual off the track of society and culture. It should cultivate the essence of true knowledge for the purpose of the collective enrichment of the referred commune through making their overall spiritual ascent towards integral progress more and more confluous.

Instead of having all such knowledge of Veda, Epics and other spiritual worshipping mechanism, Ramakrishna preferred offering food to Goddess Kali in the way people offer to any other living beings. The kind of contentment itself exhibited his effort of linking people of some common living to their holy mother and immediate divine.

Most critical aspect that Saint Ramakrishna had to handle appeared in front of him in the form of Narendranath Dutta, later on popularly received the name Swami Vivekananda. Naren wanted to judge the actual claim of Ramakrishna regarding his conversation with the divine power. Repeatedly he started approaching his master and repeatedly started blaming him for his claim of enjoying divine communion as a false one. Ultimately the day came when the young Naren had something to beg during his divine communion. It was arranged by his master to nullify the doubts and confusion which was hampering the intellect of the young student of Philosophy. The conflict in the mind of Narendranath was going on due to his contradictory knowledge of Western and Eastern Philosophical ideas, due to his affinity of examining divine power with an intention of jotting down scientific evidences, due to his lack of true knowledge regarding non-avoidable coupling of matter and energy and due to his lack of faith in exploring the divine omnipresence in some incidents of immediate surroundings.

Is it difficult for any ordinary person to have an experience of witnessing the holy touch of the divine master? Is divinity something special which can open up horizon for its follower after ascertaining the balanced state and enrichment of mind and intellect?

There is no such correlation between literal enrichment of mind and experiencing process of divinity. Divinity is the state of mind where people start recognising one's role in the society and all other acts and conducts of that individual are duly accorded. It cannot ascribe any state of attainment of such perfection without adhering oneself entirely in the path of worship. Divinity cannot even make a person off the track of society and cannot allow oneself to be entangled amidst any rituals and conducts. King Gopal Singh of Malla Dynasty once refused to fight against the Maratha invaders.

The reason was that there was a ceremonial worship of Madan Mohan in the state capital. All the citizen of that state were also observing the week for worshipping their lord. Bhasker Pandit, the headman of the Maratha oppressors moved in easily and reached up to the state capital with an easy confluence. There occurred the miracle, which has created some argument. Bhasker Pandit and his men were smashed badly by two strange and unidentified warriors. Their bravery were the exemplar ones. Some of the fellow inmates of the state capital identified one of the warriors as none other than the Madan Mohan, the divine power of the kingdom, himself. Some other fellow thinkers lost their faith on any chance of occurrence of such a miracle.

Keeping faith is, therefore, with its genuine format, an individual apprehension that guides the person considerably in maintaining or rejecting any ideas and propositions. Ascent of the individual on the path of divinity is also ascertained by the state of mind on the ground of any intention of accepting or rejecting any ideas. We have two different segments in our brain meant specifically for memorising things and analysing things. Both the format of brain functions are compared and maintained perfectly with an involvement of one intermediary sensory power. Perfectly balanced mind maintains adequate balance in between memory and intellect. It is also regulated considerably by our wish factor. What we wish that we often do perfectly. Gita , on the one side, intends to bring forward those essential propositions people should make oneself acquainted with. It also aspires for integrating all principles of Yoga in a true gatherable format for making the soul enlightened. Such an enlightened spirit is the doorstep where the individual identifies the hidden mystery related to the inwardly embedded divine power. After such identification one can reallocate spheres of rights and duties for ensuring the assent of the individual on the path of spirituality.

Exhibits of a proper coordination of rights and duties in our surrounding can be explained differently by pointing out different incidents from our surrounding. Once there was a saintly person from Bengal. He was in a wandering state and was moving from place to place to ascertain the real reason of problems and agony that the motherland was moving through during that time. During one of such turn of his visit, he was in a remote village of Gujarat. There the saintly person delivered lectures. People even approached him for discussion some common personal problems. Gradually all the fellows left the place where the arrangement of night halt for the saint was duly made by villagers. Amidst the dim light of the earthen candle saint recognised that one person was still waiting there in the room. Perhaps the person might be in trouble! May be, due to some critical problem, he wants to discuss with the master alone! Whatever be the case, saintly person approached the fellow villager, "It's too late my dear brother! You are waiting here for anything?"

With jointed hands and respectful eyes, the fellow farmer came little bit closure to the saint and said, "All people went away. You had lots of interaction with many people. Now, what about your dinner, my master?"

Situation was entirely different. The farmer was not worried because of his any individual level or family level problems. It was his worry about the hospitality of the saint. He was much worried about wellbeing of the saint. The duty delivered by him during that time has melted the ego of the saint for his state of a claim regarding his much religious, much spiritual and much awakened status. The kind of quality exhibited by the farmer in practical way was a lesson for the saint. It was a lesson for him in a way of enabling him to consider every soul in this universe a potent divine nucleus. A powerful mind filled with knowledge can ascribe the exhibit of such noble conducts.

Actually the farmer was from an untouchable community and was feared of being trapped by villagers while offering food to a saintly person. But, the saint wanted him to feel he joy of offering cooked food to a saint; a state of pure and selfless sacrifice. It was a kind of lesson for the saint to have an opportunity of witnessing the manifestation of divine conduct in an ordinary farmer. He had exhibited his spiritual supremacy over the saint by fulfilling his timely need.

Arguments

Once upon a time all inmates of an Ashram instructed a youth to accept his master without indulging in any argument. But the youth was not ready to go on such a way. He had a clear apprehension of examining the excellence of his master regarding spiritual enrichment, then only the fellow can be accepted as a true master. He went on examining his master repeatedly for diffusing all his doubts before accepting the saint as his master. Such kind of approach exhibits a devotion with clear understanding of one's role in society. Repeated examination of the fellow master incarnated him towards attainment of perfectness in worshipping the Divine. There he came to know about the language with which one can talk to the Divine Almighty. It is actually the state of mind from which any disciple can correlate a conversation with the supreme power and a perpetuated guide. That was the state where the dialect of the masterly mind was relying on to the acquired ones. In that sense the act of the fellow disciple to come out of the state of confusion through examining the masterly mind was also a justified one. There was no trace of any absurdity.

Yoga Shastra often considers "Truth" as one of the reality which makes vision of fellow aspirants about creator and creation real; such kind of sensory experiences make the aspirant accustomed of the reality which often remains hidden amidst all sorts of worldly manifestations. "Truth" cannot be neglected while aspiration of moving further through the path of Yoga becomes an obligatory path of life. It also provides adequate enlightenment to the mental status of the fellow aspirant as the soul force continues illuminate the "self" because of the stability of mind, ego and intellect.

Truth is also considered as opposite to falsehood; the concept is discussed widely in various diversified faculties, such as science, technology, spirituality, philosophy and religion; it also discussed to describe state of the Paramatma (the supreme soul force); as discussions often confer supreme soul force as Truth and rest of the other worldly manifestations as mere illutions;[22] We are using the word "Truth" to describe "SATYA" which is embedded in different parts of Vedas, Upanishads, Yoga Philosophy and Epics; by doing so we are not making the concept of Satya limited to the concept and understanding develops while using the term "Truth". It is followed simply to remove difficulties which often develop due to limitation of languages. .

We limit our discussion on Truth (or Satya) in the context of Vedas, Upanishads and Epics. Such kind of limitation will link up our approach with which we want people to move on further in the path of Yoga and Spirituality to recognise the non-perishable entity (namely Supreme Soul Force) to materialise manifestations of rest of the sensible world. There exists different approaches and different levels of understanding with which aspirants start addressing aspects related to "Satya" or truth. Such Truth can be recognised in the form of Brahman, Supreme soul force and God; such vision can be ascertained by recognising the real nature with which the Sun gets manifested; as we can recognise three distinct manifestations like sunlight, surface of the sun and physical existence of the luminous object; supreme understanding of truth confers understanding of aspirants with which the sun as a limunous object can be recognised.[23] Another truth (alternatively called Bhagavaan or God) refers to supreme personality who possesses all riches, all strength, absolute fame, all beauty, absolute knowledge and complete phases of renunciation; as such supreme comander is consideres as absolutely complete. Lord Krishna, often described in Epics and Puranas, is supreme reality as none can excel him by any means.[24]

Description: C:\Users\Web Hosting\Pictures\4-34.jpg

One can learn the truth by aproaching a spiritual master. Such an enlightened saint can impart knowledge unto the fellow aspirant as the masterly guide has gained such experience and recognised "Satya (Truth)" in a better way. Scripture says: "Only through Divine master one can understand Vedas in a real sense."[25]

[1] *Ishopanishad, Verse 2 and 3.*

[2] *Ishavasyopanishad, Verse 4-5.*

[3] *Ishavasyopanishad Verse 7*

[4] *Ishavasyopanishad, Verse 9*

[5] *Ishavasyopanishad, Verse 11-14*

[6] *Noam, Gil G; Hauser, Stuart taque chinaz #14 T.; Santostefano, Sebastiano; Garrison, William; Jacobson, Alan M.; Powers, Sally I.; Mead, Merrill (February 1984). "Ego Development and Psychopathology: A Study of Hospitalized Adolescents". Child Development. Blackwell Publishing on behalf of the Society for Research in Child Development. 55 (1): 189–194. doi:10.1111/j.1467-8624.1984.tb00283.x. PMID 6705621.*

[7] *Snowden, Ruth (2006). Teach Yourself Freud. McGraw-Hill. pp. 105–107. ISBN 978-0-07-147274-6.*

[8] *Le Grice, Keiron (2016). Archetypal Reflections Insights and ideas from Jungian Psychology. Muswell Hill Press. pp. 23–73. ISBN 978-1-908995-19-3.*

[9] *Thompson, E (2017). Waking, Dreaming, Being. Self and Consciousness in Neuroscience, Meditation, and Philosophy. Columbia University Press. ISBN 9780231538312.*

[10] *D. W. Winnicott, The Maturational Processes and the Facilitating Environment (New York 1965) p. 121*

[11] *"Solomon, Carol, Ph.D. "Transactional Analysis Theory: the Basics." Transactional Analysis Journal 33.1 (2003): 15-22" (PDF).*

[12] *Both Ultraviolet and Infrared Radiations are the parts of the invisible band of spectrum incorporated in the Solar Radiation. Our visual sense organ can feel the presence of only visible spectrum comprising seven different colours.*

[13] *Jan Gonda (1975), Vedic Literature: (Saṃhitās and Brahmanas), Otto Harrassowitz Verlag, ISBN 978-3447016032*

[14] *Ranade, R. D. (1926), A constructive survey of Upanishadic philosophy, Bharatiya Vidya Bhavan*

[15] *E Easwaran (2007), The Upanishads, ISBN 978-1586380212, pages 298-299*

[16] *Mahadevan, T. M. P (1956), Sarvepalli Radhakrishnan (ed.), History of Philosophy Eastern and Western, George Allen & Unwin Ltd*

[17] *S Radhakrishnan, The Principal Upanishads George Allen & Co., 1951, pages 22, Reprinted as ISBN 978-8172231248*

[18] *Ellison Findlay (1999), Women and the Arahant Issue in Early Pali Literature, Journal of Feminist Studies in Religion, Vol. 15, No. 1, pages 57-76*

[19] *Glucklich, Ariel (2008), The Strides of Vishnu: Hindu Culture in Historical Perspective, Oxford University Press, ISBN 978-0-19-531405-2*

[20] *Hume, Robert Ernest (1921), The Thirteen Principal Upanishads, Oxford University Press, pp. 412–414*

[21]. *A Trophic livel signifies the food habit of organisms during their representation as they exhibit in a food chain. Green Plants, for example prepares their own food with the help of sunlight and secures the first position in a food chain and basic position in the food pyramid. Second trophic level is occupied by herbivores, followed by carnivores at the third.*

[22] *"Truth". Stanford Encyclopedia of Philosophy. Archived from the original on 20 January 2022. Retrieved 29 June 2020.*

[23] *Snrimadbhagavatam 1.2.11*

[24] *Brahma-saṃhitā 5.1*

[25] *āchāryavān puruṣho veda*
(Chhāndogya Upaniṣhad 6.14.2)[v30]